Crafting
Comparison Papers

Marcia S. Freeman

Maupin House

CraftPlus
SUPPLEMENTAL RESOURCE

Crafting Comparison Papers

Cover and Book Design | Hank McAfee

Editor | Mark Devish

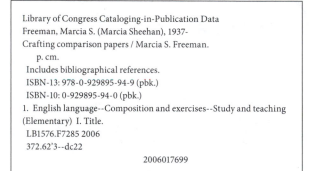

Library of Congress Cataloging-in-Publication Data
Freeman, Marcia S. (Marcia Sheehan), 1937-
Crafting comparison papers / Marcia S. Freeman.
    p. cm.
 Includes bibliographical references.
 ISBN-13: 978-0-929895-94-9 (pbk.)
 ISBN-10: 0-929895-94-0 (pbk.)
 1. English language--Composition and exercises--Study and teaching
(Elementary) I. Title.
 LB1576.F7285 2006
 372.62'3--dc22

                    2006017699

ISBN-10: 0-929895-94-0
ISBN-13: 978-0-929895-94-9

10 9 8 7 6 5 4 3 2 1

CraftPlus and Target Skills are registered trademarks or trademarks of Maupin House, Inc.

Special thanks to the administration and English faculty at O.D. Wyatt High School, Fort Worth, TX for their part in the development and application of the instructional sequence of *Crafting Comparison Papers*. Specifically, I want to thank Sherry Osman, district writing specialist, Steven Johnson, principal of O.D. Wyatt, and faculty members Mses. Miles, Cephas, Robinson, and Jacobs.

Maupin House Publishing, Inc.
PO Box 90148
Gainesville, FL 32607
1-800-524-0634 / 352-373-5588
352-373-5546 (fax)
www.maupinhouse.com
info@maupinhouse.com

Publishing Professional Resources that Improve Classroom Performance

To Mike, Michael, and Dave —
my favorite analytical thinkers

CONTENTS

CONTENTS (continued)

Preface

Over the course of my journey from biochemist and high school science teacher to elementary classroom teacher, writing-education consultant, and author, I have been intrigued by the connection between science and writing. Scientists and writers share the same types of creative bursts and many of the same skills, disciplines, and modes of thinking.

One thinking mode they share is the analytical, much of which requires, or is based upon, comparison. Comparison requires us to define, classify, and sort the entities we wish to compare; analytical thinking skills all. Teaching students how to write comparison papers is thus an excellent way to help them develop those skills.

Because all comparison is based on attributes, we start by teaching the important concept of *attribute* (an attribute is a characteristic or quality of a person, place, or thing). First, we show students how to identify and describe attributes. Next, we show them how to compare things by their identified attributes. Finally, we teach them how to apply their attribute-identification and comparison skills to writing comparison papers.

Throughout this book, you will find instruction that starts with the concrete and progresses to the more abstract. I think Jean Piaget would have liked this. His insights into children's mental development have guided me in codifying my science and writing education philosophies and practices. If you have not read Piaget's work, I urge you to do so. You will then understand why and how I have applied his principles to writing instruction.

You have probably heard the expression "Writing is thinking." After reading this book and applying its principles and practices in your classroom, I am confident you will more fully appreciate the validity of that proposition. And you will see how learning the craft required to write comparison papers develops, nurtures, and utilizes analytical thinking.

Marcia S. Freeman
AUGUST 2006

CHAPTER 1
Introduction to Teaching Comparison

❯ The Educational Power of Comparison

"Of all the instructional strategies that positively affect student achievement, helping students *identify similarities and differences* had the largest average effect" (Robert Marzano in *What Works in Schools: Translating Research into Action,* 2003).

Wow! Not the instructional strategies of cooperative learning, summarizing and note taking; not questions, cues, and advance organizers; not homework and practice or setting objectives and providing feedback; but helping students identify and describe similarities and differences. In other words: *teaching students the craft of comparison.*

This research finding alone is a compelling reason to devote a portion of our writing instruction time to comparison. Moreover, *comparison* has broad and frequent application in the learning process across the curriculum. From fourth grade and up, we frequently expect and demand that students write comparison papers. We know them to be an excellent content-assessment tool. Additionally, performance-based reading tests often include comparison tasks, both through extended answers and analytical essays.

❯ Comparison Defined

Webster's *New World Dictionary* defines *compare* as *to examine for similarities and differences.* It defines *contrast* as *to compare in a special way, which is to display differences.*

In spite of this dictionary definition, and because we hear the phrase *compare and contrast* used so often, we tend to infer that *compare* means to find only likenesses. Not so. *Compare and contrast* is a redundancy. In this book, I stick to the dictionary meaning. Whenever I use *compare* or *comparison* you will know that I am referring to looking at both likenesses and differences.

❯ Comparison Papers

Comparison papers involve identifying and describing the similarities and differences of two or more things based on multiple attributes. Such papers serve at least one of two basic functions: informing and persuading. For example, by comparing two biomes, we can inform our readers about the characteristics of each. By comparing two musical performances, we can attempt to establish the superiority of one over the other and try to persuade the reader of that superiority.

The opportunity to write comparison papers arises frequently across the curriculum. Think of comparison papers students might be assigned in science, history, and geography: *Compare the tundra and prairie biomes. Compare the causes of WWI and WWII. Compare the coastal regions of Virginia and Florida and explain how that geography affected their subsequent development.* Math, art, and music all offer opportunities for comparison as well: *Compare a hexagon to a pentagon. Compare Monet's and Van Gogh's brush techniques. Compare rap and poetry.*

And don't forget English class assignments that call for comparisons of text. During research projects, students need to compare and evaluate the validity and usefulness of information sources. And when analyzing fiction, students compare settings, plots, characters, motives, and themes.

> Teaching Comparison

Instruction in the craft of comparison, as is the case with teaching all aspects of writing craft, must be explicit if it is to be effective. That is, we must teach the specific set of writing-craft skills associated with comparison. The traditional assign-and-assess approach to writing does not and cannot foster writing competency.

The methodology in this book is based on the principles and practices of CraftPlus®, my craft-based, school-wide writing instruction program. If you are familiar with those principles and practices, you will already understand some of the specific terminology I use throughout this book, such as *Target Skill, models, genre blocks, Student Writing Notebook, Teacher Writing Instruction Notebook,* and *Target Skills™-based assessment.* Even so, you may want to read the *Quick Review of CraftPlus* in Appendix 1 (page 62) before you proceed with the steps in the instructional sequence.

If you are not already familiar with CraftPlus principles and practices, you definitely will want to read **both** the *Quick Review* and *A Crash Course in CraftPlus* in Appendix 1 before undertaking the instruction outlined in chapters 2-5.

Who Teaches How to Write a Comparison Paper?

Classroom teachers in grades 4 and 5 and language-arts or English teachers in grades 6-12 are responsible for teaching students how to write comparison papers.

Language-arts teachers should work in synch with their content-area colleagues (science, geography, math, history, art, music, and literature) so they'll know what comparison-based papers those colleagues will be assigning and when they plan on assigning them. They can then coordinate their scheduling of comparison-paper instruction so that students can use their content-area topic for material as they write during the lessons. This cross-curricular cooperation has a powerful educational impact.

Content-area teachers should be conversant with the lessons in this book so that when they assign comparison papers they use consistent terminology and methodology when helping students apply comparison tools and techniques.

When Is Comparison Taught?

All teachers in grades 4-12 have a role to play in comparison instruction. Fourth-grade students are capable of learning basic comparison-craft skills and using them to educational advantage. Middle and high school students are able to handle more advanced craft skills, and their larger vocabulary and increased content knowledge allows them to apply their skills at increasing levels of sophistication. There are ample opportunities, and an increasing need, for them to do this across the curriculum.

Ideally, your school will have adopted a progressive writing curriculum (such as the one in CraftPlus) so that you eventually will be able to rely on most of your incoming students having mastered the requisite set of precursor skills for your grade. If your school has not done this, you will have to adjust the content and pace of your instruction to match your students' writing experience and their prior knowledge and facility in comparison, especially in the craft of identifying and describing attributes.

> The Instructional Sequence

The instructional sequence for teaching the crafting of comparison papers is composed of four steps:

- Step 1: Identifying and describing physical and abstract attributes; writing a descriptive paragraph.

- Step 2: Using a graphic organizer to compare by multiple attributes.

- Step 3: Writing a comparison paragraph using cue words.

- Step 4: Organizing and writing a multi-paragraph comparison paper.

These four steps are covered in chapters 2-5, respectively. Each chapter includes background information, specific lessons, and models for teaching the writing-craft skills. Included also are a suggested timeline for the instructional sequence, the order in which to perform lessons, and examples of student writing produced in response to the lessons.

Each of the four instructional steps consists of a sequence of lessons presented over consecutive days. Each step includes time for students to practice the lesson skills and an assessment of the students' ability to apply the skills in a piece of writing.

> Note that students will be keeping Student Writing Notebooks (loose-leaf notebooks with tabbed sections). As the instructional sequence progresses, your students will store their reference lists, writing ideas, lesson notes, and practice writing in their Student Writing Notebooks.
>
> In later writing-craft lessons, students will revise the pieces they've saved by incorporating the new skills. This practice helps students understand revision for what it is—making something better, not correcting errors. (It also saves time during writing-craft lessons.)

I call the first, third, and fourth steps of the instructional sequence *genre blocks* because, following instruction and practice in the addressed genres of description (Step 1) and comparison (Steps 3 & 4), each student writes a piece, either a paragraph or a multi-paragraph paper, and submits it for assessment. (See Appendix 1, page 62, for a more complete discussion of genre blocks.)

The objective for the end of Step 2 is not a written piece but the completion of a *comparison graphic organizer,* which is submitted for assessment. Students will subsequently use such organizers as a prewriting tool in the comparison-paragraph and comparison-paper genre blocks.

Step 1: Description Genre Block—A Precursor Skill to Making Comparisons

Technically, *description* is not a genre, but for purposes of this book I treat it as a genre. Whatever we call it, description is a significant writing skill that is supportive of almost every other genre.

Writers describe people and things using a vocabulary associated with attributes. They describe physical characteristics (*size, shape, color, age, texture,* etc.) of people and things, as well as more abstract qualities such as *honesty, durability,* and *reliability.* Because it focuses on attributes, description is an important precursor to comparison. That is why description is the first of the four steps in the instructional sequence of crafting comparison papers. You will use this description genre block to review and extend the crucial concept of attribute. (See Chapter 2: Identifying and Describing Attributes.)

At the end of the block, your students will write a descriptive piece and submit it for assessment.

NOTE: Language arts teachers commonly follow description with a Personal Narrative Genre Block, during which students apply the descriptive skills they have just learned. Personal narrative is an engaging genre, since students are writing about themselves. By immediately following description with personal narrative, you can hook students into your writing program.

Step 2: Graphic Organizers—A Prewriting Tool

In the second step of the instructional sequence you will show your students how to use graphic analyzers as prewriting tools. Following lessons and practice, they will demonstrate their facility in using a graphic tool to compare two or more entities.

This step should be scheduled whenever you are ready to conduct a comparison-paragraph genre block or a comparison-paper genre block (Steps 3 & 4). Students will use comparison graphic organizers to pre-write as they plan their genre pieces. (See Chapter 3 for lessons about graphic prewriting tools.)

Steps 3 and 4: Comparison-Paragraph and Comparison-Paper Genre Blocks

The third and fourth steps in the instructional sequence are genre blocks. At the end of the third step, students submit a comparison *paragraph* for assessment. At the end of the fourth step, they submit a multi-paragraph comparison *paper* for assessment.

What Does an Instructional Block Schedule Look Like?

In each chapter you will find a graphic like the one pictured at the top of page 5. These graphics show the consecutive days of an instructional block. (The sample provided is from Step 3: Writing a Comparison Paragraph.) These graphics are accompanied by advice about compressing or extending the block depending on your students' facility with the lesson skills.

How Are the Instructional Steps Scheduled?

Step 1, Identifying Attributes and Description, should always be the first writing instruction of the school year. Students will be able to use the descriptive-writing composing skills they acquire in this block not only for the comparison genre but also for every genre you address over the course of the year.

The subsequent steps do not need to be scheduled immediately after the first step. In the interim—after completing Step 1, but before starting the rest of the instructional steps for teaching comparison—you may teach general writing-craft lessons such as literary devices, beginnings and endings, and supporting details, and genres such as personal narrative or informational reports.

Further into the school year, when you are ready to address comparison, you can proceed with Step 2 (Graphic Organizers) and Step 3 (Comparison Paragraph), one right after the other.

After you have completed Step 3 in the instructional sequence for teaching comparison, you may decide your students need additional instruction and more practice in creating organizers and writing comparison paragraphs. For this additional instruction, repeat some of the lessons in Steps 2 and 3, choosing different topics, or use some of the optional lessons you will find in the chapters. When your students can competently compose comparison paragraphs, you can proceed to Step 4 and have them tackle a whole comparison paper.

Day 1	*Lesson 1: Cue Words for Comparison*	Whole-class participation in creating a list of cue words.
Day 2	*Lessons 2: Using Cue Words in a Comparison Paragraph*	Model how to use cue words within a paragraph. Use one of the class-generated graphic organizers from Lesson 2 in Chapter 3. Students each write a paragraph using their graphic organizers from that lesson.
Day 3	*Lesson 2 (cont): Review and Practice*	Students write another comparison paragraph with cue words, using a previously constructed *Comparison Analysis Organizer* or after creating a new one. **Homework Journal:** Target Skill: using cue words to write a comparison paragraph.
Day 4	*Lesson 3 (Grades 4-8): Conventional Comparison Paragraph Text Structure*	Model the conventional format. Students identify the conventional format in texts. Students write a paragraph using the conventional format and cue words.
Day 5	*Lesson 4 (Grades 6-8): Exception to Conventional Format*	Students identify the alternative format (attribute-by-attribute) in text. Students write a paragraph using the alternative format. **Journals returned.**
Day 6	*Evaluation piece*	Assign or have students select a pair to compare. Students generate a *CraftPlus Comparison Analysis Organizer,* then write a comparison paragraph using cue words. **Paragraph due** at end of period.

If you have students who have already had instruction and practice in writing comparison paragraphs, you can schedule Step 4, Writing a Comparison Paper, right after Step 2, Using a Graphic Organizer. Take your students through Step 2 to be sure they know how to use the Comparison Analysis Organizer (a modified Venn diagram discussed in Chapter 3), then go directly to Step 4.

Are the Genre Blocks Repeated in the School Year?

Teachers in grades 4-12 should schedule **at least two** comparison units after completing instruction in or a review of the graphic organizers presented in Step 2. For example:

Fourth and fifth grades: One or more **comparison-paragraph** genre blocks and one multi-paragraphed **comparison-paper** genre block. It would be best for students to select their own topics so you can be assured they have good control over their subject matter.

Sixth, seventh, and eighth grades: One **comparison-paragraph** block (for students who have not previously had this instruction) and two multi-paragraphed **comparison-paper** genre blocks. The comparison papers may be associated with a content area such as literature, science, or history.

Ninth through twelfth grades: Two or more multi-paragraphed **comparison-paper** genre blocks. Review using a comparison analysis organizer and writing comparison paragraphs with cue words. The papers may be associated with a content area such as literature, science, or history.

> The Lessons

In each of the chapters devoted to the steps in the instructional sequence, I describe the essential lessons for the instructional step and optional lessons that can extend it.

The lessons I present can be used in grades 4-12. While the student-written models I have included come predominantly from grades 4-8, high school teachers have used these lessons effectively by increasing the breadth and sophistication of vocabulary and content-area application—with, of course, increased expectations.

If comparing texts is an academic requirement or is pertinent to state testing in these grades, comparison genre blocks should be devoted specifically to comparing texts. Appendix 3, Comparing Texts, contains information specific to that task and includes detailed lists of text attributes. These include physical, genre-specific, and writing-craft attributes.

What Does a Lesson Look Like in a Forty-Minute Class?

In each chapter you will find graphics similar to the one following. (The sample is from a lesson in Step 3: Writing Comparison Paragraphs.) These graphics represent the procedural portion of a lesson. They fit a forty-minute class session.

Description of the lessons is provided in the chapter text, as are models you can use with those lessons. (Appendix 1 has more details about lessons and lesson plans.)

40-minute class	Instructional Procedure and Student Response: Lesson 1 Target Skill: Cue Words for Comparison
20 minutes	Introduction: Review the concept of cue words by referring to narrative time-and-place cue words. Introduce comparison cue words. Help students construct a class list of words that alert readers to similarities and differences. Students copy list to retain in their writing notebooks.
10-15 minutes	Show Student Model: Show the students the model provided for this lesson. Have them check it against what they listed. Provide them with a thesaurus for further investigation of cue words.
5 minutes	Students share findings. Store list in their writing notebooks.

Using Literary Models

Literary models for attributes abound. Illustrated children's books are amazingly useful as models at all grade levels when working with attribute identification and vocabulary. Older students can readily understand the content and they seem to enjoy these books as much as their younger counterparts do.

Literary models of comparison **papers** are relatively difficult to find. Comparison is not a common organization scheme of published books. (See the Bibliography for children's books that can serve as models for the comparison genre.) You are more likely to find models for comparison papers in magazines.

Models for comparison as an organizational scheme for **paragraphs** (text structure), however, are more available and can be found in many non-fiction books and magazine articles.

One of the CraftPlus core resources, *Models for Teaching Writing-Craft Target Skills* (see Bibliography on page 60), provides lists of both trade books and books published by educational publishers that you can use for models when you teach comparison craft skills as well as for the other genres and skills you teach in your writing program.

Using Student Writing as Models

One of the best sources of models is your own students' writing. The samples provided in this book will serve as your first models, but over time you will want to collect your own students' writing to use as lesson models. Among the models I have included in this book is a student's assessment piece for each of the four instructional steps.

This icon 📄 will tell you that there is a reproducible graphic available in Appendix 4. Feel free to reproduce these graphics to share with your students or use them to make overhead transparencies.

> Assessing Student Writing

At the end of each chapter devoted to an instructional step (chapters 2-5), you will find a sample rubric similar to the one following. You can use such rubrics to assess your students' achievement in relation to the lessons you have taught. You may need to revise this rubric to match the rubrics used in your school district.

📄 For a blank version of this rubric, see Reproducible #1 in Appendix 4.

Sample Assessment Rubric (See other examples in Appendix 1):

Comparison Paragraph—Target-Skill Application	3 Applies skill creatively and competently	2 Applies skill competently	1 Attempts to apply skill	Not scoreable
Identifies attributes of the things compared.				
Uses comparison cue words.				
Presents text in a consistent format (similarities then differences or attribute by attribute).				

> Remember

At each step of the following instructional sequence (chapters 2-5), you will find optional lessons to reinforce the skills of the step. You can use them to adjust the length and order of your instructional blocks to accommodate your students' background experiences in identifying attributes, using graphic organizers to make comparisons based on multiple attributes, and applying writing-craft skills.

CHAPTER 2
Step 1: Identifying and Describing Attributes

Comparison lies at the heart of much of our analytical thinking. Throughout our lives we compare, often subconsciously, new things we encounter with the things that we already know. It's one of the ways we learn. Attributes, both concrete and abstract, lie at the heart of all comparison. Thus to rationally and effectively make comparisons, we have to master the precursor skill of *identifying attributes.*

As toddlers we based many of our early comparisons on physical attributes we could perceive with our five senses—properties such as *color* and *shape.* We extended and refined our concept of *bird* by comparing each new bird we saw with birds we had seen before. As we acquired language skills, we learned the names of these attributes and the attribute classes to which they belonged. For example—*yellow*, a color; *long and pointy*, a shape.

As adults we continue comparing things based on physical attributes, but we also learn to base many of our important comparisons on more abstract characteristics. We compare characters in books based on their actions. We compare and evaluate sports or music performances based on the skills and artistry displayed. We compare the principles and ideas of competing candidates to decide whom to vote for. We compare climates, employment opportunities, and lifestyles offered by various locales to determine where to live.

The ability to identify and describe *attributes* is the single most important precursor skill for writing comparison papers.

> Attribute Defined

The American Heritage Dictionary defines *attribute* as *a quality or characteristic inherent in or ascribed to someone or something.* We can identify attributes by perceiving them through our senses, or we can ascribe them based on evidence, prior experience, and judgment. Most attributes can be measured, some on an absolute scale (*miles per gallon, temperature*) and some only on a relative or qualitative scale (*pale red, highly unpleasant, very risky*).

Attributes range in a continuum from the concrete to the highly abstract. Concrete attributes include those that we can perceive directly through our senses: *color, texture, odor, pitch, saltiness,* and *weight.* Abstract attributes include such things as *risk, honesty, efficiency, durability,* and *social prestige.* (Understanding and identifying abstract attributes requires a greater degree of life experience, logical reasoning, or personal judgment than are required for concrete attributes.)

When students identify attributes, they should learn·to identify attributes from all along the continuum. Younger students will certainly tend to stay near the concrete end of the continuum, but older students will identify and describe increasingly abstract attributes.

A hierarchy of attributes starts with broad general categories that are progressively subdivided into increasingly specific subclasses and, ultimately, into highly specific characteristics or properties. For example, one attribute of animals is its *physical appearance.* More specifically, one attribute of physical appearance is *covering material.* More specifically, chicken's *feathers*, dogs' *fur*, and snakes' *scales* are their covering materials and are attributes specific to those animals.

Learning about attributes is largely a matter of becoming aware of, and learning the vocabulary associated with, the specific *properties* and *characteristics* of people, places, and things, and the attribute classes to which they belong.

Because primary grade teachers devote a good deal of time teaching students how to sort and classify, most students will come to your class understanding that attributes can be sorted and classified—that *red*, *blue*, *green*, and *pink* are *colors*, or that *bones*, *muscles*, and *tendons* are *body parts*.

The goal of your instruction is to teach your students how to identify a larger number of abstract attributes and the words that describe the classes into which they sort and classify them. For instance, they will learn that character traits such as *honesty, reliability*, and *trustworthiness* can be grouped into a category of attributes called *personality traits*.

Reinforcing the Concept of Attribute

In the classroom, you can reinforce the concept of *attribute* by using attributes as the basis of how your students line up, choose partners, sort themselves into groups, and the like. For example: "Everyone with the attribute of *blue eyes*, (or *black hair, wearing jeans*, or *with a green backpack*) get your writing folder from the bookcase," or "I'd like everyone with the attribute of a *one-syllable first name* in this group." If you always use the word *attribute* as you direct your students, they will acquire a full understanding of the meaning of the word without your ever having to define it explicitly. (This is, by the way, the natural and predominant way we learn language.)

Because *observation and description* is the classic starting point in the scientific process, your students will likely be studying or reviewing the properties of matter and materials in science class as well as in your writing program. You should alert your school's science teachers to the attribute-identification work you are doing at the start of the year so that they can reinforce the concept in their teaching and in the science writing they will require of your students.

The Vocabulary of Attributes

To describe things accurately, writers need a substantial descriptive vocabulary. We must help students build this vocabulary throughout all grades.

Primary students start with descriptive words for basic *physical attributes*, such as *color, number, texture, shape, pitch, and location.*

Older students continue to expand their vocabulary of physical attributes and learn the concepts and vocabulary of *abstract attributes*, such as *honesty, efficiency*, and *risk*.

The vocabulary of attribute description is not limited to adjectives. Writers use nouns, strong verbs, adverbs, and literary comparisons as well. You can describe an animal by saying it *has* a certain feature, such as *fur* (noun). You can describe the way something moves with the word *stealthily* (adverb). You can describe the character trait of *honesty* by saying *the person is an Abe Lincoln* (metaphor).

When we do use adjectives, we often can choose from three categories: *specific, non-specific*, or *comparative*. For example, to describe *size*:

- specific (determined by measurement): *0.2 inches long*

- non-specific: *small*

- comparative: *pea-sized* or *smaller than a pea*

William Shakespeare coined hundreds of words. Astoundingly, as Bill Bryson notes in *The Mother Tongue* (1990), of the 17,677 different words Shakespeare used in his writing, at least one tenth had never been used before. Many of these new words stuck and enrich our language today. Language is always a work-in-progress. For example, a made up, non-specific word for size is *ginormous*—a blend of *gigantic* and *enormous*.

> Attribute Lists

📄 You will find the following starter lists of attributes and their associated vocabularies useful as you implement the lessons in this chapter. Included are sample lists of attributes associated with various content areas such as math, geography (maps), science, and literature. The lists should provide students with enough examples for them to generalize about attributes and associated vocabularies. See Reproducibles #2–9 in Appendix 4.

Students can and should add to these lists. In general, lists generated by student writers themselves, as a result of their reading, are always more useful to them than any we might give them. To that end, before you reproduce any of the lists for your students, you might tape over or white out some of the entries for each listed attribute, leaving room for students to enlarge the lists with their own vocabulary.

NOTE: Make copies of these attribute lists and give them to your students to keep in their writing notebooks.

Sample List of General Physical Attributes and Associated Vocabulary

NOTE: This list includes attributes that can be quantified by measurement or judgment to be more descriptively precise.

movement or **action**: gliding, slithering, flapping, explosive; *comparative*—faster, more frenzied

number: *specific* (through measurement)—fourteen, a thousand; *non-specific*—many, some, several; *comparative*—more than, fewer, as many as a baseball team **size**: *specific* (through measurement)—nine-by-twelve inches, one-hundred yards; *non specific*—large, huge, tiny; *comparative*—larger, as big as

color: purple, green, pale yellow; *comparative*—reddish, sea green

shape: round, oval, cubic, square, columnar, tubular, triangular; *comparative*—box-like, pie shaped

texture: smooth, rough, bumpy, lumpy, soft, fuzzy, slippery; *comparative*—stickier, slickest

special features: written, knobbed, patterned, ribbed, buttoned, zipped

location: under, over, behind, beside, far away; *comparative*—closer, farther away

direction: left, right, up, down, backward, forward

temperature: *specific* (through measurement)—forty-six degrees, three below zero; *non-specific*—broiling, freezing; *comparative*—hotter than, coldest

weight: *specific* (through measurement)—ten pounds, seven grams; *non-specific*—heavy, light; *comparative*—as heavy as, the lightest

age: *specific* (through measurement)—five years old, eighteen months old; *nonspecific*—old, new, ancient, antique; *comparative*—older than the hills

smell: smoky, putrid, floral, acrid, burnt, sweet; *comparative*—like smoke, like burned rubber

taste: sweet, salty, acidic; *comparative*—like licorice, fruitier

sound: *specific*—bass, treble; *non-specific*—loud, soft, grating; *comparative*—high-pitched, low-pitched, raspy, whistling, humming, melodic

state: liquid, solid, gas

symmetry: horizontal, vertical, radial

habitat: underground, den, water, ocean, desert, forest, tundra

orientation: horizontal, vertical, parallel, perpendicular

composition: wooden, metal, plastic, cloth, glass, concrete, cardboard, paper

Sample List of Character Traits

physical or **behavioral**: aggressive, agile, boisterous, bookish, calm, clumsy, confused, dignified, energetic, fearless, foolhardy, fragile, fussy, gregarious, handy, hardy, headstrong, illiterate, insane, lazy, likable, literate, mealy mouthed, polite, poor, powerful, punctual, reclusive, relaxed, rude, sarcastic, serene, shy, stingy, sturdy, tall, thin, timid, unkind, verbose, vulnerable, weak, weary

emotional: afraid, angry, annoyed, anxious, ashamed, cheerful, confident, content, creative, delighted, depressed, down, elated, excited, frustrated, furious, glad, guilty, happy, hateful, helpless, hostile, hurt, insecure, irate, irritated, jealous, joyful, lonely, melancholy, morose, optimistic, pessimistic, proud, sad, satisfied, scared, thankful, unhappy

moral or **ethical**: calculating, conceited, cowardly, deceitful, dishonest, faithful, false, honest, honorable, generous, loyal, reliable, trustworthy, sneaky, steadfast, untrustworthy, wishy-washy

Sample List of Science Attributes (Properties of Matter and Material)

appearance: physical attributes (*see above*)

state: liquid, solid, gaseous

plasticity: brittle, stretchy, bendy, rigid, pliable, flexible

hardness: as hard as a diamond, slate-like, malleable

density (weight per volume): *comparative*—denser than balsa wood, as light as aluminum, thicker than oil

buoyancy: floats like a cork, sinks like lead

conductivity: resistance, as conductive as copper, insulated

viscosity (liquids—as compared to a standard): flows faster than molasses, as thick as oil, runny like water, gooey as glycerin

miscibility: dissolved in oil, water, glycerin, alcohol, layered like oil on water

reactivity: oxidized, corroded, rusty, etched by acid, inert

Sample List of Botany Attributes

leaf edging: lobed, serrate (*like saw teeth*), smooth

leaf surface texture: hirsute (*hairy*), glabrous (*smooth, shiny*)

leaf and bud position: opposite, alternate, whirled

venation: pinnate (*like a feather*), palmate (*like a hand*)

stem: scaly, smooth, hirsute, sticky

fruit type: drupe, berry, pod, capsule, samara, nut

flowers: regular, irregular; solitary, compound, composite, in clusters, in catkins, in panicles, in umbels, in spikes, in heads

sepals and petals: inferior, superior

Sample List of Animal Attributes

features: antennae, beak, bill, ears, feathers, four–legged, fur, invertebrate, microscopic, pileated, pupate, scales, segmented, shell, spotted, striped, thorax, toes, tongue, two–legged, vertebrate, whiskered, winged

behavior: arboreal, aquatic, carnivorous, cold-blooded, domesticated feral, ferocious, herbivorous, insectivorous, larval, omnivorous, predatory, solitary, warm-blooded, wild

Sample List of Map Attributes

physical features: borders, compass rose, contour lines, elevation, grid lines, latitude, longitude, legend, projection, scale, sea level, symbols, topography

land forms denoted: mesa, valley, river, dam, lake, mountain, outcropping, plain, plateaus, mountain range, swamp, bay, coastal flood plain, peninsula, delta

political features and subdivisions: boundaries, state capitals, major cities, counties, township, population

Sample List of Text Attributes   (*See also Appendix 3: Comparing Text*)

features: art illustrations, charts, close-ups, cross sections, text density, diagram, font size, font styles, glossary, graphs, headings, illustrations, index, insets, labeled photographs, lists, maps, paragraph length, photos, schedules, table of contents, tables

genre attributes: purpose, content, text structure, arguments, characters, setting, plot, motive, theme, transitions

writing-craft attributes: anecdotes, ending techniques, hooks, onomatopoeia, metaphor, irony, anadiplosis, synecdoche, repetition, quotations, specificity, strong verbs, dialog tags, voice

Sample List of Math Attributes

geometric: parallel, perpendicular, conical, triangular, oval, rhombic, rectangular, cylindrical, round, square, two dimensional, three dimensional, solid, plane, oblong, perimeter, area, volume, closed, connected, bounded, concave, convex, regular, symmetrical

numerical: negative, positive, integer, numerals, fractional, real, rational, irrational, whole, part, proper fractions, improper fractions, few, many, some, thousands, a google

algebraic: equality, inequality, variables, quadratic, sets, greater than, less than

measurement: *weight*—heavy, light, scaled, pounds, ton; *length*—long, short, inches, centimeter, meter; *capacity*—full, empty, milliliters, cups, gallons, liter, milliliter

> The Descriptive Writing Genre Block

Writers identify and describe attributes to create imagery for their readers. With this in mind you should start the school year in all grades with descriptive writing instruction. The initial lessons in this genre block are about attributes. As a result of this instruction your students will not only be developing their descriptive powers, but also the attribute-identification skills and associated vocabulary they will need in order to write comparison paragraphs and, ultimately, comparison papers.

During this instructional period your students will

1. identify physical and abstract attributes

2. add to their attribute vocabulary

3. practice descriptive writing

4. write a descriptive piece for assessment

The genre block sample provided here is based on a 10-day schedule. Depending on your curricular needs and your students' ages and experience, you can extend this instructional period with further lessons about attributes and their relationship to descriptive writing (see **Optional Lessons** on page 20). You can also use these optional lessons for review throughout the year.

While the genre block schedule is the same for all grades, the content of the lessons will vary depending on the attributes you choose as Target Skills and the entities students analyze for attributes. This content must match the vocabulary and interests of your students.

> Since good descriptive writing includes literary comparisons, you may also want to teach your students, or review with them, the various ways authors compare one thing to another. This will extend the genre block by several days. (See Appendix 2: Literary Devices on page 70.)

In the last day or two of the genre block students should be ready to write a descriptive piece for assessment. They will have participated in your lessons and will have had ample practice identifying attributes through lesson responses, homework journals, or from content areas. They will take this descriptive piece through drafting, revising to the Target Skills of the block, and editing. The topic of the writing assessment for genre pieces may be selected by the students, suggested by a picture from the class collection, or provided by you in the form of a written prompt.

See Reproducible #10 in Appendix 4 for an example of a student-written descriptive genre-block piece.

Remember that all the time parameters throughout this book are suggestions only. In this sample 10-day genre block you will see that the final class period is set aside for writing the assessed piece. If you estimate that your students need more time than this to complete it, add another day to the block. Please proceed at a pace that is appropriate for you and your students.

Day 1	Lesson 1: Attributes in Description	A basic Target Skill lesson using sensory attributes to describe a picture. Students write a paragraph describing a picture using sensory attributes.
Day 2	Simulation of a Peer Conference	Peer responder identifies and compliments writers' use of the Target Skill. Students write a paragraph selecting a set of sensory attributes to describe a photo, then peer conference.
Day 3	Lesson 2: Colors	Students will work in groups to brainstorm color vocabulary: using a variety of materials. **Homework Journal**—Target Skill: color vocabulary
Day 4	Lesson 3: Map Attributes	Whole-class exercise on identifying map attributes. Students list attributes of their own maps.
Day 5	Lesson 3 (cont)	Model writing a paragraph to describe a map. Students write a paragraph to describe their own maps, referring to attributes. **Homework Journals returned**.
Day 6	Lesson 4: Character Traits	Model how to describe person or book character. Students list attributes and then write a paragraph describing a person or book character.
Day 7	Lesson 4 (review)	Model describing a real person or a book character. Students write a paragraph describing a person or book character. Meet with groups for review of attribute identification.
Day 8	Lesson 5: Consistent Presentation Format	Model orally the consistent format or presentation. Students practice selecting and using a format to describe a picture orally (any attributes). **Homework Journal**—Target Skill: Character traits as attributes. Students write to describe a person or book character.
Day 9	Review of Targeted Punctuation, Capitalization, or Grammar Convention (Grade-Appropriate)	Students edit each other's practice writing or journal writing for the convention Target Skill of the block. (See Appendix 1 for a discussion of convention Target Skills.)
Day 10	Evaluation Piece	Students write a page-long descriptive piece. (Allow them to use lesson notes.) Draft, revise to Target Skills and edit for the targeted writing convention of the block. **Descriptive piece due** at end of period. **Journals returned**.

⟩ The Lessons

Lesson 1: Attributes in Description

a) Using the basic Target Skill lesson description in Appendix 1 (see page 62), show your students how to use specific attributes in description. Select two to four attributes from the *Sample of General Physical Attributes* list (Reproducible #2). Select attributes that are appropriate to your students' experience and vocabulary range. For example:

> Describe the colors in a picture: *Monet's use of muted but natural earth tones sets his work apart from Van Gogh's.*

> Use a number word: *Thirty percent of the student body has enrolled in the Renaissance Program.*

> Use a size word: *Light heavyweights dominated the schedule on "Saturday Night at the Fights."*

b) Provide each student with a copy of the *Sample of General Physical Attributes* list or an abridged version you may have prepared. Ask students to select a picture from the class collection. Read from children's literature to model how writers use the vocabulary of attributes. *Models for Teaching Writing-Craft Target Skills* (see Bibliography on page 60) provides lists of such literature, both fiction and non-fiction.

c) Orally model a description of a picture you show them, focusing on two to three physical attributes. As you model the paragraph show students how you use a writing convention (capitalization, punctuation, or grammar) that you have selected as a Target Skill focus for the block.

Ask students to do the same for their pictures, describing them to partners and focusing on the attributes they selected. Then have them write their descriptions. Allow time for them to share their writing with others. Ask peer responders to compliment writers for their use of attribute vocabulary by attaching stickers or placing color symbols directly on the writer's work.

Sample Forty-Minute Lesson Model

The chart at the top of page 16 suggests a sequence and time requirement for the lesson procedure. You can use it as a model when you plan the additional lessons you select and conduct during the block.

🖹 Rebekah described a photograph of a green snake by focusing on two attributes (Reproducible #11).

Lesson 2: Colors

This lesson is an example of one of the many ways to help students build their descriptive vocabulary. Depending on the age and experience of your students, you may vary the content attribute of this Target Skill lesson.

a) Words for colors are virtually limitless and most of them have a name. Use the biggest box of Crayola® crayons to demonstrate the variety. Show students how many color names derive from comparisons to natural elements, such as flowers, trees, and woods—*periwinkle blue, coral, primrose, lemon yellow, mahogany, sky blue, orchid, ash blond, etc.*

40-minute class	Instructional Procedure and Student Response: Lesson 1 Target Skill: Attributes in Description
15- 20 minutes	Introduce *attribute* as a Target Skill. Give each student the list of physical attributes and have them select a photo from the class collection. Ask students to read the list to themselves or have volunteers read it aloud to class. Read to the class a few pages from a children's book or poem that illustrates many descriptive adjectives (a *model*). Ask students to listen for the attributes the author describes (color, size, movement, number). Show them your picture (overhead slide or large picture). Tell them the three attributes you have selected as Target Skills, and then orally model how you describe the picture based on these three attributes. (Include the use of the convention selected for the block.)
5 minutes	Students try it out (orally): Have students select 2-4 attributes they will focus on, and then ask them to describe their photos to partners using the vocabulary of the attributes they selected.
10 minutes	Students write a paragraph of description with the attributes they selected as the Target Skills. Encourage students to list, as a simple prewriting tool, some of the attribute vocabulary they will be using. Circulate around the room and help student writers by asking them to articulate sentences they plan to write (*guided writing*).
5 minutes	Have students share their writing with a partner. Peer responders should compliment the use of attribute vocabulary. Writers store practice piece in their writing notebooks.

Bryan created a collection of words describing the color white.

Bryan
Gr 6 per 6

cream, eggshell, ivory, ecru, lily, alabaster, irredescent, blinding, dingy, vanilla

eraser, styrofoam, whiteout, smoke, powder, fog, baking soda, frozen, grape, mist, salt, frost, whitehouse, light, blizzard, candle, wick, bone, polar bear, wax, guano, sand, coral, candle, galaxies, stars, napkin, baby wipe, piña colada, toilet paper, light bulb

Provide color-word resources for students. Ask your art teacher for other sources in addition to the following:

- Crayola® crayons: box of 64
- paint chips: dozens of cards each with an array of six to eight named shades of one color are available at home improvement, paint, and hardware stores
- carpet and towel ads
- new-car color charts from local car dealers

b) In partnerships or groups, students brainstorm lists of descriptive words for several colors. In the last ten minutes of class, ask them to share their work with the class or with one another. Have students save this practice writing in their writing notebooks.

Always be aware that when students share their examples during these lessons, they are teaching each other.

Homework option: Have students create a collection of color words in notebooks. Provide for their sharing the results as well as their sources.

Lesson 3: Map Attributes (Session One)

📄 a) Provide students with a collection of grade-appropriate maps. Ask students to contribute to the collection if possible. (See sample maps, Reproducibles #12 and 13). Using a pull-down map or a projection of a map by overhead transparency, guide your students to construct a class list of map attributes. Record their suggested attributes on chart paper, overhead transparency, or through computer technology. Seed the class' list using some of the attributes from the *Sample List of Map Attributes* Reproducible #7.

Students will need instruction in order to articulate some of the attributes. For example, if they notice the different colors for states and county borders and list attributes of *black lines* and *blue dotted lines*, a discussion—and possibly some research—about what the lines denote will help them express the more abstract attribute of *political subdivision*.

b) Next have students list the attributes specific to their own maps. Circulate and help them articulate the terms for attributes. Give them time to share their lists and to discuss the different maps they have collected. Direct them to store their lists for tomorrow's work.

In preparation for session two, prepare student copies of the class-generated list of map attributes. Add attributes from the list provided in this chapter if they were not included.

Lesson 3: Map Attributes (Session Two)

a) Model for your students how to write a paragraph describing the attributes of a map. As you model, tell them that you are placing sentences containing information about related attributes in close proximity to each another. Explaining the logic of your presentation when you model is always desirable.

b) Provide students with the class-generated list of map attributes that they created in the first session. Then have your students check their maps for attributes from the list they may not have found in the previous session. Have them write single-paragraph descriptions of their maps, referring to as many attributes as they can. Do not require or expect graceful writing—the object of this lesson is only to identify and describe map attributes.

Students should save these lists of attributes and their maps for the work they will do later in Step 3 of the instructional sequence.

The following charts suggest a sequence and time requirement for the two-session Lesson 3 procedure.

40-minute class	Instructional Procedure and Student Response: Lesson 3 Target Skill: Identifying Attributes of Maps
15- 20 minutes	Session 1—Introduction to map attributes: Give out copies of several different maps. Allow 5 minutes for students to look over their maps. Tell them the object of the lesson is to construct a class chart of map attributes. Guide them to form a list comparable to the list of map attributes provided in this chapter. (You can give them an abbreviated version to serve as a seed list.)
15-20 minutes	Students try it out: Have the students list the attributes specific to their own maps.
5 minutes	Share: Have students read their list to a partner and put it in their writing notebook.

40-minute class	Instructional Procedure and Student Response: Lesson 3 (continued) Target Skill: Identifying Attributes of Maps
10-15 minutes	Session 2—Review of map attributes: Give out copies of the class-generated Map Attribute list. Ask for volunteers to read the list. Ask for any additions. Model how to write a paragraph describing the attributes of the projected map or class map. As you model the paragraph, tell your students that you are placing sentences about related attributes in close proximity.
15-20 minutes	Students try it out: Have your students write single-paragraph descriptions of their maps, referring to as many attributes in their text as they can. Do not expect graceful writing, the object of this lesson is to identify and name map attributes.
10 minutes	Share: Have students read their paragraphs to two other students. Circulate to hear the results yourself. Ask peer responders to put a color mark as a compliment for each attribute the writer identified as he described his map. Have students save their lists, maps, and paragraphs in their writing notebook.

📄 Until you have collected samples from your students, you may use Reproducible #14 and 15 as models for your instruction.

Lesson 4: Character Traits

a) Provide your students with the *Sample List of People or Character Traits* (Reproducible #3). Have them read it over (aloud or silently). Then read a familiar children's book (*Peter Rabbit, Amelia Bedelia,* a Miss Nelson book, *Alexander and the Wind-Up Mouse, The Magic Pebble, Mike Mulligan and Marianne* or another of your favorites) to your class. Ask the students to listen for character descriptions as you read the entire story. Have students raise their hands when they think they heard the author revealing or describing a character. Discuss what trait or attribute they think it is. Have a class scribe keep a list of the student observations on an overhead transparency or through computer technology.

b) After the reading, project the list for the class to see. Ask students to write a paragraph describing a character in the book. Have them share their work with two other students. Ask responders to recommend paragraphs they heard that they think the class should hear.

Lesson 5: Consistent Organizational Format

When writers describe characters, places and events they help their readers visualize. They also help their readers remember the people, place, or events by presenting the information in a consistent sequence. They may first focus on movement (strong-verb writing), then gracefully work in other attributes. Their guiding rule is not to jump back and forth between attribute types or elements in a scene. Readers find such jumping around disconcerting and confusing. They need descriptive text to be presented as logically as informational text or essays.

This list of ordered presentation formats is available as Reproducible #16.

> **People**: physical attributes first then emotional or vice versa, faces before the rest of the person, action before physical features
>
> **Setting**: from one element in the scene to another; from left to right; from top to bottom; from the central figure out; from foreground to background
>
> **Events**: chronological order

a) Give your students a copy of Reproducible #16. Then read (aloud) some short, descriptive passages from fiction or non-fiction. Help your students analyze a variety of passages to identify the consistent presentation format an author followed.

Model the following examples:

> **Emotion the Character Displayed, then Physical Attributes:**
> Hattie smirked and her high cheekbones jutted up toward her eyes. Her skin was dark brown like her mother's and looked smooth under the yellow streetlights.
> (from *Last Summer with Maizon,* Jacqueline Woodson,1990)
>
> **Top to Bottom:**
> All rain forests grow in layers. The top layer, the canopy, is the roof of the forest. It consists of the tops of trees. The understory is beneath that. This part of the forest is made up of palms, short trees, and other plants. The forest floor is the bottom layer. The plants here are not thick because they get very little sunlight.
>
> **From One Element to Another:**
> Addie knew instantly that the big easy chair across from the sofa was Uncle Henry's. His pipe and glasses sat on a small table beside it, and a newspaper was folded on the floor. The old oak rocker, which had been in Grams family for many years, had been brought down from the farm. It reminded Addie of all the times she had rocked on Gram's lap. The rocker stood now near the big window with Gram's knitting basket close beside it on the floor.
> (from *Oonawassee Summer,* Melissa Forney, 2000)
>
> **Chronological Order of Events:**
> She baited her hook with a big, juicy worm. She pulled the fishing line away from the polished pole between the reel and the first loop. The line unwound smoothly and silently from her new reel. She flicked the baited book back and forth, swishing it in a big arc over her head. She was ready at last. She swung the hook out over the pool beneath the bridge.
> (from *Catfish and Spaghetti,* by Marcia S. Freeman, 1998)

b) Model (orally) how to describe a person or a scene in a photograph, using one of the presentation formats. As you do it, tell students what you are thinking as you construct the piece so that they can see the choices you made to follow a format. Can they identify which one you are modeling?

c) Have students work in pairs, each student with a picture of his own, to orally describe a scene in their pictures to their partner. Call for volunteers to describe their pictures in a consistent format to the class. Either ask each volunteer to name the format he or she used, or ask audience students to identify it.

In a second session or for homework, ask students to write the description. The Target Skill is *using a consistent presentation format.*

> Optional Lessons

Optional Lesson A: Floor Plans—Attributes of Housing

📄 Make a transparency of the floor plan provided as Reproducible #17. Show it to your students and discuss some of the attributes of an apartment, house, or condo. List those attributes on the overhead transparency and leave it up for students to see (*number of windows, square footage, number of closets, orientation of rooms or components of rooms*).

Provide your students with copies of the two floor plans provided in Reproducible #18. Have the students (working in partnerships or individually) identify and list the attributes of each of the two apartments they have. Students should save this list for the work they will do later: writing a paragraph using comparison cue words (see Chapter 4).

Optional Lesson B: Innovation on **The Important Book**

The Important Book, by Margaret Wise Brown, first published in 1949, is enjoying a renaissance, as teachers from fourth to eighth grade have discovered what a wonderful model it is for describing the *essential attributes* of an object. If you attend a state reading association conference you are likely to find a session in which a teacher will demonstrate how they use this book to help students identify main ideas and details.

Brown's text follows this pattern: *The important thing about the sky is it is blue. Large fluffy clouds form in it. Birds fly in it. Trees grow up into it. It's always there when you look up. But the most important thing about the sky is it is blue.*

Show your students how to write text like this, using common objects such as shoes, hats, umbrellas, and toys. In educational parlance this emulation technique is known as *innovation.* When students have mastered the pattern, have them all read a small non-fiction piece in a content area they are studying (weather, whales, whatever) and identify the important things (attributes) about the topic of the text. Then have them write a paragraph about that topic emulating the style of *The Important Book.*

After they are able to handle this exercise, have them create their own "important book" in response to their current studies in science, social studies, math, or art, for you to use as an authentic assessment piece.

📄 Justin innovated on *The Important* Book to define *tundra.* His writing sample is Reproducible #19.

Optional Lesson C: Attribute Show-and-Tell—Oral and Written

The day before this lesson, ask your students to bring in objects that match a topic or theme associated with their current studies in science, history, literature, art, math, or music. Divide the class into groups of three or four and have each group select one of the objects and then list as many of its attributes as they can identify. Invite each group to report to the class the attributes they identified, either in list form or in sentences that incorporate the attributes.

Before asking students to do this, model some sentences for them about an object. For example:

> Object: A horseshoe
>
> Attributes: *composition, surface texture, color, weight, use, age, shape, pattern of nail holes*
>
> Sample sentences: *This horseshoe is about as heavy as Joe's shoe. We are guessing it is made of iron or steel. A series of holes follows the U-shape of the shoe. It's used to protect a horse's hoof from wear and tear on pavement or gravel.*

This exercise can be practiced as a written assignment in their homework journals as well.

Optional Lesson D: Attribute Field Trip

Take your students on an "attribute field trip" in the school halls or schoolyard to identify and describe attributes. Language-arts field trips are as valuable as science and social studies field trips.

Procedure:
Provide students with clipboards and the *Sample List of General Physical Attributes* (Reproducible #2).

Model one or two entries about the target attribute on the board before leaving the classroom. For example, your might give some examples of shapes and composition to get your students started. *The trophy case in the front hall is square and the trophy plaques are mostly rectangles. The cafeteria garbage pails are cylinders and made of plastic.*

If you change the Target Skill to *describing attributes by comparison*, your examples might be: *The silver trophies are as shiny as car bumpers. The cafeteria trays are so grungy the germs are probably complaining.*

At the end of the field trip, have your students share their work.

Optional Lesson E: Textures

Have students create a collection of textures. Samples can be mounted on card stock. Make a class chart of words to describe these textures. Use students' own words first, even made-up words. Keep the chart as a work in progress, with students adding to it as they discover further texture words in their reading. Place a student's initials after a contribution to the chart. Publish the charts on 8 ½" x 11" papers for students to keep in a writing notebook.

Optional Lesson F: Describing Sounds

Compared to visuals, we have a limited vocabulary for sounds. One way we extend this vocabulary is by making up words that imitate sounds: *Splash, whir, pbzzt, kerplop,* etc. This is called *onomatopoeia.* For a literature model of vocabulary for the attribute of sound, even older students will enjoy Peter Spier's onomatopoeia books, *Crash! Bang! Boom!* and *Gobble, Growl, Grunt.*

We can describe sounds by their source and intensity as well as their quality. Take your class outside for a sound field trip. Seat the class in a comfortable, shady spot and ask the students to identify one or two sounds they hear. *Can you describe the sound? Where does it come from? Is it loud or soft? Is it pleasant or is it annoying? Is it a humming or whistling sound? Is it high-pitched or low?* You should do this as an oral exercise. Alternatively, coordinate this lesson with the music teachers.

Ask students to write a paragraph describing the sounds they heard.

When you read to your students, bring it to their attention whenever an author uses onomatopoeia. Invite students to use sound words in their writing.

Optional Lesson G: Practicing Scientific Description

Observation and description are among of the most important skills that scientists use. By helping students become adept at observation and description we can prepare them for studying science over the rest of their lives. We also will have made them better writers and better thinkers. You can promote and reinforce your students' observation and descriptive skills as follows.

Create a classroom collection of science-theme pictures, or collect *National Geographic* magazines and science journals that contain articles about the science topics your students will study during the year: *insects, plants, ocean life, rocks, weather phenomenon, land forms, biomes (habitats), planets, etc.*

Model for the students how to identify definitive attributes about an object, animal, or place. For example: *a Zebra—black and white stripes, a short mane, black hooves, large rounded ears like a rabbit, found wild only in Africa,* etc. Have students contribute attributes about your model subject. List the attributes and leave the list up for students to see.

Have each student select a different object, place, or animal and list its definitive attributes. Then ask them to write an "All About *X*" (where *X* = the topic) booklet for an audience of younger children. They should devote each page of the booklet to a particular *attribute* of the topic. They should write descriptive text for each topic-related attribute: *color, location, size, shape, food type, etc.* They may use photos or their own drawings to illustrate the book

Post the content words for the chosen topics and make correct spelling of the content words the editing standard for the project. Arrange for your students to read their booklets to groups or classes of younger students.

Optional Lesson H: Identifying Math Attributes

Lead a brainstorming session to create a list of math vocabulary that your students know. Then have them select pictures from the class collection and, as a prewriting exercise, have them list the mathematical terms that can be applied to the objects in their photographs. Help them identify which of those terms are attributes.

Samples of math attributes:

- a *diameter* is an attribute of a circle

- a *right angle* is an attribute of a right triangle

- *parallelism* is an attribute of train tracks

- *number* is an attribute of a herd or flock of animals

- *sides* are an attribute of a polygon

Students can list descriptive (physical) attributes of pictured objects as well. Provide a model for them. For example, show them a picture of a pencil. Their attribute list might include *six parallel sides, yellow color, lead is cylindrical shape with conical point, metal trim or band at end, about 90% of the pencil is composed of wood,* etc.

Optional Lesson I: Describing Geometric Attributes

You can integrate geometry and writing by using plane and solid shapes as a source of descriptive vocabulary. Check with the math teacher to learn in what marking period this geometry topic is studied, as well as what geometric shapes will be studied. Do this lesson concurrently to reinforce the concepts and vocabulary of attributes.

With the class, create a list of geometric shapes, angles, and other related concepts (such as *diameter, arc, diagonal*) that the students know or are studying.

Next, model how to talk about geometric shapes found in nature, architectural environments, and such. Do this by orally describing a photo in an overhead projection.

> *I see a triangular shadow cast on the ground by the batting cage.*

> *The angle between the football blocking equipment and the ground is less than 90 degrees.*

Now have the students each select a picture from the class collection and ask them to write a descriptive paragraph about the geometric attributes found in their photos.

Homework Journaling Option: Ask students to find and describe geometric shapes in their home or neighborhood environments.

> Assessment

The assessment criteria for the descriptive piece students write at the end of the genre block are the Target Skills you have taught and your students have practiced during this instructional period. Your objective is to evaluate how well (using a numerical or letter scale) they are able to use the specific skills.

Sample Assessment Rubric (See other examples in Appendix 1):

Description— Target-Skill Application	3 Applies skill creatively and competently	2 Applies skill competently	1 Attempts to apply skill	Not scoreable
Uses a consistent format.				
Uses vocabulary of various sensory attributes (assigned or self-selected).				
Identifies and uses vocabulary appropriate to learned attributes.				
Uses grade-level convention: capitalization/ punctuation/ grammar.				

> Remember

Comparison is based on identified attributes. Before you ask your students to write comparison papers on any topic, make sure they have a good grasp of the attribute concept and have developed a good working vocabulary for describing attributes.

CHAPTER 3
Step 2: Comparing One Thing with Another Using a Graphic Organizer

Making comparisons is a critical thinking skill. Mastering that skill will not only lead students toward proficiency in writing comparison papers, but also in analyzing problems, making decisions, and evaluating the variety of situations and documents they will encounter in school and beyond.

After you have gone through Step 1 of the instructional sequence (see Chapter 2) your students will have a significant understanding of the attribute concept and a working attribute vocabulary. They will be ready for the next step: comparing one thing with another to show similarities and differences, and making that comparison based on multiple attributes.

❯ The Role of Graphic Organizers

Identifying, analyzing, and organizing multiple attributes of two things to be compared is a relatively complex task. The task is facilitated by using tools such as graphic organizers. Simple graphic tools such as a flipbook or T-chart are introduced to students in the primary grades. More complex ones, such as Venn diagrams, modified Venn diagrams, and matrices are appropriate from fourth grade and up. These graphic tools are all used in the prewriting process. (You will find a lesson that reviews using flipbooks as a graphic tool on page 31.)

❯ A Modified Venn Diagram

Traditionally, we have asked student writers to use the classic Venn diagram as a prewriting tool for comparison. When used for prewriting, the Venn diagram usually comprises two overlapping circles, each circle representing a physical or logical entity. The overlapped areas represent the attributes those entities have in common. (See Optional Lesson C: Matrices on page 32 for information about comparing more than two things.)

Although logically apt, a classic Venn diagram (see below) is inconvenient for comparison prewriting. This is because writing in the circular spaces is often difficult, and writing in the narrow elliptical space formed by two overlapping circles is downright awkward.

Fortunately, there is no rule that says we have to use overlapping circles in a Venn diagram. So for comparison prewriting, I instead use two overlapping rectangles, which makes the overlapping area a rectangle as well. More importantly, I add a fourth, left-hand column, labeled "ATTRIBUTES." I call this modified Venn diagram the *CraftPlus® Comparison Analysis Organizer*.

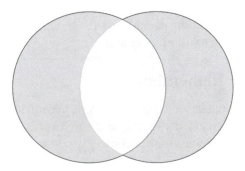

The format of this organizer greatly facilitates the attribute-by-attribute analysis students need to complete when we ask them to write comparison papers in any content area. You can make the columns of the rectangular organizer as wide as you like. Outlining the two rectangles in different colors is helpful. (Using curved corners reminiscent of circles can also help students adjust to the new configuration.) The CraftPlus® Comparison Analysis Organizer looks like this:

CraftPlus® COMPARISON ANALYSIS ORGANIZER

ATTRIBUTE	X	BOTH	Y

📄 See Reproducible #20 for a blank copy of this organizer.

An Important Note on Using Comparison Organizers

When comparing one thing with another, we must compare them attribute-by-attribute. It is of no value to say something like, "A cat has whiskers, but a dog barks." This means that when we use a comparison organizer, we must arrange it and fill it in attribute-by-attribute. We cannot randomly list the characteristics of *X*, then the characteristic of *Y* while throwing in a few *Boths* as we go. We have to address one attribute at a time as we analyze, filling in the pertinent information for *X*, *Y*, and *Both*. The left-hand column of the CraftPlus Comparison Analysis Organizer makes this easier.

> Share the CraftPlus Comparison Analysis Organizer with your colleagues in the various content areas and encourage them to use it in their classes. Point out that it can serve both as an instructional aid and as an authentic assessment tool—if students can identify both similarities and differences on the organizer, you can be assured they probably have a significant level of knowledge of the subject.

› The Instructional Block

The objective of this second step in the instructional sequence is developing your students' ability to use a graphic organizer to compare two things by multiple attributes. The Target Skills of the lessons in this block are those required to achieve this objective. Students will apply these skills when they pre-write at the start of both the Comparison Paragraph and the Comparison Paper genre blocks, the third and fourth steps in the instructional sequence.

During this second step of the instructional sequence, your students will

    a. identify multiple attributes

    b. add to their attribute vocabulary

    c. practice comparing pairs of things using a graphic organizer

    d. compare two items by multiple attributes using a CraftPlus Comparison Analysis Organizer for assessment

The instructional block sample provided here is based on a five-day schedule. You can extend it with further lessons as the needs of your students dictate. You will find **Optional Lessons** starting on page 30.

Day 1	*Lesson 1: Identifying Pairs-to-Compare*	Review of attributes. Model likely Pairs-to-Compare. Students, in groups, list likely pairs of things to be compared.
Day 2	*Lesson 2: Using the CraftPlus Comparison Analysis Organizer*	Model filling out a Comparison Analysis Organizer for the attributes of ducks and chickens or using a pair about which your students have a great deal of knowledge.
Day 3	*Lesson 2 (cont)*	Review and practice. Students, in partnerships, use a Comparison Analysis Organizer to compare two things by multiple attributes, selecting from the Pairs-to-Compare lists or a pair you provide. **Homework Journals—** Compare a pair using organizer.
Day 4	*Lesson 2 (cont)*	Review and practice using a Comparison Analysis Organizer. Students (solo) practice using a Comparison Analysis Organizer to compare a pair of their own choosing.
Day 5	*Assessment*	Assign students a pair to compare (from a topic area they know well) and have them fill out a CraftPlus Comparison Analysis Organizer. **Journals returned**.

> The Lessons

Lesson 1: Identifying Pairs to Compare

a) As a class exercise, have students offer some examples of pairs of things they have been called on to compare in or outside school (two different TV programs, sports, science habitats, etc.). List their input on the board.

Then, ask the students what they notice about these pairs. (The answer you're looking for is that the two things in each pair share many of the same attributes.) If no one notices the shared attributes, ask them if they think it would be likely (or useful) for someone to ask them to compare *a piano and a banana*, *a boat and a thistle*, or *a cat and a battery*. They should quickly come to the conclusion that it would not be very likely. Ask them why not. (The answer is that since these pairs share almost no attributes other than both being solid matter, comparing them is not useful or meaningful.)

b) In groups of three or four, have students identify and list pairs of things they think it would be reasonable to compare (meaning pairs that have some attributes in common). Contemplating what pairs to compare reinforces the concept of *attribute* and develops facility in recognizing and identifying attributes.

Before they begin, model the start of a list of some likely pairs selected from all content areas of the grade curriculum. The list should include processes and events as well as objects and people. Some possible pairs include

- damselflies and dragonflies
- skunks and raccoons
- Frost and Whitman
- Othello and Hamlet
- marimba and piano
- painting and sculpting
- Van Gogh and Renoir
- policeman and fireman

- hawks and eagles
- kayaking and rowing
- Melville and London
- playing a flute or a trumpet
- guitar and banjo
- watercolors and pastels
- decimals and fractions
- WWI and WWII

Sharing: Ask each group to select a reporter and have each reporter read her group's list of pairs to the class.

c) After all the groups have been reported, have each student copy several pairs from his group's list to his own paper. Then have each student identify two to three attributes shared by each pair on his list. Invite the students to share this information with the members of their original group.

Students should retain the written responses to this lesson for use in subsequent lessons. They should keep the lists in their writing notebooks and add to it whenever they like.

Sample Forty-Minute Lesson Model

The following chart suggests a sequence and time requirement for the Lesson 1 procedure.

40-minute class	Instructional Procedure and Student Response: Lesson 1 Target Skill: Identifying Pairs-to-Compare
10 minutes	Introduction: Lead a discussion of likely pairs to compare in a variety of content areas—concept of shared multiple attributes. Show examples of pairs not likely to be compared.
10-15 minutes	Students try it out: Students work in small groups to produce a list of Pairs-to-Compare.
10-15 minutes	Student groups report pairs, then list attributes: Groups report their lists, and students copy entries onto their own lists. Then they list 2-3 attributes shared by each pair.
5 minutes	Students share: Have students share their lists with members of their group, then put their lists in their writing notebooks.

Pairs to Compare

alligators / crocodiles
dogs / wolves
seagulls / pigeons
pen / pencil
Adding / subtraction
water / ice
Apples / oranges
tile / carpet
Shoe / sock
Soccer / Kickball
Ketchup / mustard
door / window

Student-Writing Model for Lesson 1:

📄 Jasmine, a fifth-grader, responded to this lesson. Her Pairs-to-Compare (Reproducible #21) can be used as a model.

Lesson 2: Using the CraftPlus Comparison Analysis Organizer

This lesson and its practice writing can be conducted over two to four class sessions, depending on your students' facility with identifying multiple attributes and making comparisons.

Provide each student with a blank copy of a CraftPlus Comparison Analysis Organizer (Reproducible #20). Then, in a whole-class exercise, model how to use this graphic tool to do a attribute-by-attribute analysis.
📄 Use the following ducks and chickens model, also available as Reproducible #22, or use a pair taken from the class Pairs-to-Compare list from Lesson 1.) Have the students supply the organizer entries while you act as scribe, guide, and encourager.

CraftPlus® COMPARISON ANALYSIS ORGANIZER

ATTRIBUTE	ducks	BOTH	chickens
Voice	quack	produce sounds	peep, cluck
Ability to swim	swim well	are able	swim poorly
Mouths	bills(rounded)	hard material, upper & lower	pointed beaks or slightly pointed
Classification		Aves: birds, fowl; Vertebrates	
Reproduction		lay eggs	
Egg size	size of an oval tennis ball		smaller than duck's
Covering		feathers	
Colors	brown, white, varied	many	red, black/white, buff, white, variegated.
Comb	no comb		red comb
Wattle	under beak		no wattle
Feet	webbed toes		separate toes
Body temperature		constant, warm blooded	
Diet	water plants, crustaceans, fish, berries	insects, plants, seeds	grain
Habitat	wild: ponds, wetlands, domestic: farms		farm, free or caged
Flight	good at it, high		awkward, low

Please remember, the models presented here are suggestions only. You and your students may want to use a different pair. Encourage your students to choose something familiar to them. (See the Student-Writing Models at the end of this lesson—page 30.)

b) After the whole-class interactive model, ask students, in partnerships, to do a similar analysis of a pair they select from one of their own Pairs-to-Compare lists (or a pair you provide from one of the content areas).

For example:

Science: living things (horse and zebra), habitats (tundra and desert), chemicals (hydrogen chloride and acetic acid), materials (aluminum and brass), rocks (slate and marble)

Music: instruments (flute and clarinet), music genres (country western and bluegrass), musical groups (jazz trio and marching band)

Art: media (pastels and charcoal), techniques (impressionist and cubist), artists (Monet and Van Gogh)

Math: operations (addition and multiplication), geometric forms (sphere and dodecahedron), processes (finding area and finding volume)

Geography: water forms (lake and pond), land forms (canyon and valley), maps (geophysical and topographical)

Social Studies: historical eras (The Great Depression and World War II), political or historical events (Pearl Harbor and 9/11), people in history (Lee and Grant), states (Vermont and Maine)

NOTE: For students whose learning mode is primarily concrete and visual, the maps and floor plans provided in Chapter 2 will be of great use. Additionally, photo pairs help these students identify attributes and make comparisons.

c) After completing an analysis with a partner, ask students to do this exercise solo, with newly selected pairs. Circulate around the classroom and provide guidance as needed.

> Finding the words to identify attributes—particularly abstract attributes—is the most difficult part of comparison for students. It requires that they look beyond physical or sensory attributes. For example, when analyzing ducks and chicks, students need to consider attributes beyond the birds' colors and the noises they make. They have to identify such things as their taxonomic classifications, habitats, or domestic uses. Explicit instruction and lots of practice is a must.

After students have taken part in the instructional model, done an analysis with a partner, and performed a solo analysis in class with your guidance, they should be familiar enough with the process to use the graphic organizer independently. At this point you can ask them to do one for assessment.

Have students save their filled-in organizers so that they can use them for planning comparison paragraphs or multi-paragraph papers in the next two instructional steps detailed in chapters 4 and 5.

Sample Forty-Minute Lesson Model

The following chart suggests a sequence and time requirement for the Lesson 2 procedure.

40-minute class	Instructional Procedure and Student Response: Lesson 2 Target Skill: Using the CraftPlus Comparison Analysis Organizer
25 minutes	Introduction: Model how to compare two items, attribute by attribute, using a *CraftPlus Comparison Analysis Organizer*. Students provide entries to chart.
15 minutes	Students try it out: Students start, in partnerships, to compare a selected pair, analyzing the two by multiple attributes.

Student-Writing Models for Lesson 2

Until you have collected samples from your students use the following student responses to this lesson as models for your instruction.

📄 Rebekah used attributes to compare two salads. See Reproducible #23. Chris identified attributes in order to compare basketball and soccer. See Reproducible #24.

This whole-class analysis was constructed by third-grade students and their teacher.

CraftPlus® COMPARISON ANALYSIS ORGANIZER

ATTRIBUTE	geranium	BOTH	cactus
Chlorophyll		all green plants have	
Leaves	curly edged leaves		no leaves, bumpy sections
Texture of leaf	soft and hairy		no leaves
Water need	Almost daily water	both need water	little water, grows in desert
Stems	have stems		no stems or maybe it's all stem
Spines	None		many
Flowers		have	
Flower color	Red		yellow
Roots	roots long	have	roots short, shallow.

> Optional Lessons

Optional Lesson A: Pairs Unlikely to be Compared

Ask students, in groups, to list pairs that are unlikely to be compared because they share so few attributes. As a model, first assess a few such pairs in a class discussion: for example, *piano and banana, boat and thistle, cat and battery*. Have each group reporter read the group's unlikely pair list. This usually leads to some humorous pairings, or mis-pairings.

Make a game of this activity by challenging students try to find common attributes for each unlikely pair offered by the presenting group. Any pair for which the rest of the class can identify two or more attributes is disqualified, and the group that offered it has to find a more unlikely pair.

Just as writing badly on purpose can help us learn to write better, this exercise can reinforce students' understanding of the concept of common or shared attributes.

Optional Lesson B: Flipbooks

A flipbook is a simple fold-and-cut paper model that can be used to compare two things with each other based on several attributes (up to four attributes if students use an 8½ by 11 sheet of paper for the chart). It is often used to introduce graphic organizers to younger students, but high school students have used it to quickly compare *Othello* and *Hamlet*.

<u>To Make a Flipbook</u>

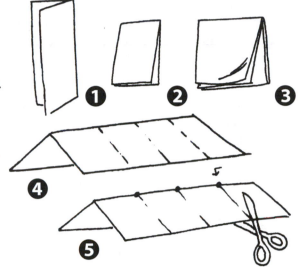

1. Fold an 8½" by 11" sheet of paper longwise.

2. Fold that in half, top to bottom.

3. Fold that in half again in the same direction.

4. Open the paper and drape it over your arm lengthwise.

5. Cut up along the fold lines on one side, only as far as the lengthwise fold.

6. Now you have four flaps. You use the graphic with the rectangular flaps in a vertical or horizontal aspect.

<u>Using a Flipbook</u>

As a whole-class lesson, select a grade-appropriate pair of things to compare, such as *flute and trumpet*, *Spanish and English*, *tundra and savannah*, *triangle and rhombus*. Prepare a large paper model of a flipbook for your demonstration.

Model how to compare the selected pair by several attributes. Ask students to compose very simple statements that show the similarities and differences between the pairs based on those attributes. Enter the simple statements in your model flipbook. Enter the statements about one of the pair on the top flap and enter the statements about the other in the corresponding rectangles beneath the flaps.

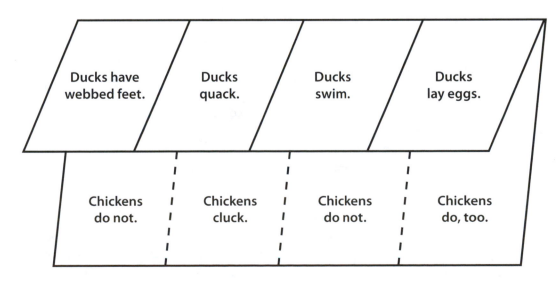

A fourth grade class composed as it compared ducks and chicks.

Ask your students to do the same for a pair they select from their Pairs-to-Compare lists from Lesson 1. Students can write in these flipbooks in the vertical or horizontal aspect. Provide time for them to share their work with others.

Homework: Have your students create a series of these booklets across many topic areas for ample practice. The booklets should be saved for subsequent lessons about using comparison cue words in writing cohesive comparison paragraphs (described in Chapter 4).

Optional Lesson C: Matrices

Comparing three or more things with one another is a much less common school task. If and when students are asked to perform it, a graphic organizer called a matrix will help them. The rows of a matrix usually represent the things being compared, and the columns designate the attributes. There is no limit to the number of things or attributes that may be compared. With your help, students should be able to create matrices in any of the content areas.

Begin by modeling how to use a matrix such as the one below. For your model select examples of multiple things from a content area, such as literature, science, music, or social studies. Some examples: several characters in a book, science materials, wars, colonies, states, musical instruments, etc.

Then ask your students, in partnerships, to select a content area and do the same kind of analysis for three or four items within that content area.

Models for Optional Lesson C

A Sample Comparison Matrix for Analyzing the Attributes of Musical Instruments

Instrument	made from	physical description	sound-production means	solo or group instrument	kind of music or groups
Clarinet	wood or metal	long, black tube with a reed mouthpiece and holes the length of the tube.	blowing through a reed mouth-piece	solo and group	dance band, symphonic, jazz groups. Rare in county music.
Tuba	metal	large, brass, curled, with large mouth.	blowing through a cup like mouthpiece, using lips to control air.	group more usual	marching band, symphonic
Guitar	wood, metal, or plastic	hour glass shape with a hole in center, strings running from bridge over hole to pegs at top.	plucking or strumming strings with fingers or pick.	solo and group	varied: jazz, blues, country, Latin, classical

A Sample Comparison Matrix for Analyzing the Attributes of Materials

Object	composition	treatment of light	absorbency	texture	flexibility	buoyancy

> Assessment

The assessment criteria for this instructional block are the Target Skills that you have taught and your students have practiced during this instructional period. Your objective is to evaluate how well (using a numerical or letter scale) they are able to use the specific skills.

Sample Assessment Rubric (See other examples in Appendix 1):

Comparison Using a Graphic Organizer— Target Skill Application	3 Applies skill creatively and competently	2 Applies skill competently	1 Attempts to apply skill	Not scoreable
Identifies and names the attributes by which to compare two things.				
Writes appropriate information about similarities and differences in the graphic organizer.				

> Remember

Students need ample opportunity to practice using a comparison organizer as a pre-writing tool. They will quickly learn how helpful it is for organizing a comparison **paragraph** or comparison **paper** on any topic.

Using the CraftPlus Comparison Analysis Organizer has a five-fold educational impact. It

- provides a pre-writing tool for comparison
- improves writing organization and clarity
- fosters content learning
- provides content-area teachers with an authentic assessment tool
- develops analytical thinking

CHAPTER 4
Step 3: Writing a Comparison Paragraph

Since good writing instruction always proceeds from simpler skills to more complex ones, we should teach students how to write a single paragraph before we teach them how to write a multi-paragraph paper. The lessons of this chapter are designed to show students how to construct a single paragraph of comparison text structure using cue words. In Chapter 5 you will see how the principles and skills for writing a comparison paragraph apply to writing a multi-paragraph comparison paper.

› Text Structure and the Writing-to-Reading Connection

Text structure refers to the organizational scheme of a paragraph. It is the way a writer has chosen, for that paragraph, to show readers the relationship between the facts or ideas presented. Some commonly used text structures are: description, comparison, contrast, process or procedure sequence, definition, main idea and supporting details, main idea with multiple examples, cause and effect, and problem and solution.

Your students should have been, or are currently being, introduced to paragraph text structure through guided reading of non-fiction and informational texts. Once your students are able to recognize text structures in their reading, it is time to teach them how to create text structures in their writing. You will find that when students can construct text structures in their writing they are better able to comprehend them in their reading.

Reading researcher T. Shanahan (1997) points out that close connection between writing and reading. He noted that, "Awareness of an author's choices is central to effective critical reading, but this information is well hidden in text, and children become aware of it rather late in their development. Writing, because it affords one an insider's view of this aspect of text, provides a powerful, complementary way of thinking about reading that would not be available if reading and writing were identical."

This feedback loop between reading and writing exists for every writing-craft skill. That is, student awareness of writing craft increases their engagement with text they read, as they start reading not only for content but for craft as well.

› Cue Words

Alerting the Reader to the Text Structure

Cue words, also known as transitions, help writers lead their readers clearly from one fact or thought to another, both *within* and *between* paragraphs. Cue words tell the reader how what he has just read is connected or related to what is coming.

Your students may have had previous instruction in the use of cue words. They should be familiar with time and place transitional cue words, which are an integral part of writing-craft instruction in the narrative genres.

Comparison Cue Words

Cue words such as *both*, *unlike*, and *similarly* tell the reader that the relationship between facts and ideas is one of comparison. These cue words are used within paragraphs as well as between paragraphs. Using such cue words within paragraphs is the focus of the Comparison-Paragraph Genre Block that composes the third step of the instructional sequence.

❯ The Comparison-Paragraph Genre Block

The third step in the comparison paper's instructional sequence is a genre block. At the end of it students will write a comparison paragraph for assessment.

During this instructional period, your students will

    a. continue to identify physical and abstract attributes

    b. add to their cue word vocabulary

    c. practice writing paragraphs with a comparison text structure

    d. write a comparison paragraph for assessment

The genre block sample provided here is based on a five- or six-day schedule. You can extend it by having students practice writing more comparison paragraphs or with further lessons about cue words and contrast text structure (differences only). See **Optional Lessons** on page 40.

Day 1	*Lesson 1: Cue Words for Comparison*	Whole-class participation in creating a list of cue words.
Day 2	*Lessons 2: Using Cue Words in a Comparison Paragraph*	Model how to use cue words within a paragraph. (Use one of the class-generated graphic organizers from Lesson 2 in Chapter 3—see page 28.) Students each write a paragraph using their graphic organizers from that lesson.
Day 3	*Lesson 2 (cont)*	Review and practice. Students write another comparison paragraph with cue words, using a previously constructed Comparison Analysis Organizer or after creating a new one. **Homework Journal**—Target Skill: using cue words to write a comparison paragraph.
Day 4	*Lesson 3 (Grades 4-8): Conventional Comparison-paragraph Text Structure*	Model the conventional format. Students identify the conventional format in texts. Students write a paragraph using the conventional format and cue words.
Day 5	*Lesson 4 (Grades 6-8): Exception to Conventional Format*	Students identify the attribute-by-attribute alternative format in text. Students write a paragraph using the alternative format. **Journals returned.**
Day 6	*Evaluation Piece*	Assign or have students select a Pair-to-Compare. Students generate a CraftPlus Comparison Analysis Organizer, then write a comparison paragraph using cue words. **Paragraph due** at end of period.

› The Lessons

For the lessons in this block, students will need the Pairs-to-Compare lists they compiled and the CraftPlus Comparison Analysis Organizers they constructed during Lessons 1 and 2 in Chapter 3.

Lesson 1: Cue Words for Comparison

a) Review the concept of cue words in general, by discussing the use of time-and-place cue words in narrative (*later, after that, suddenly, meanwhile back at the ranch*). Ask students, "How do time-and-place cue words help the reader? What do they alert the reader to?" (The answer you are seeking: the reader can keep track of the chronology of events and where the characters are.)

b) Next, introduce cue words writers use to alert their readers to similarities and differences. Rather than simply giving your students a list of these cue words, you will find it more useful and effective to have them create one themselves. Do this in a shared writing experience.

Get them started by seeding the class list with one or two cue words from the list provided here. Record their contributions on chart paper or on an overhead transparency. Suggest an additional cue word or two when they run out of ideas. Usually this evokes a few more student suggestions. Have the students copy the list as the class builds it.

Examples of Comparison Cue Words:

• both	• like	• unlike	• similarly
• but	• different	• the same as	• on the other hand
• in a similar fashion	• as with	• just as	• in contrast
• whereas	• rather than	• however	• analogous to

📄 c) When the class list is finished show them Iane's Cue Words for Comparison (Reproducible #25). Have them check for any words they omitted. Have them retain the completed list in their writing notebooks. Encourage them to add to it when they find additional examples in their independent reading.

Sample Forty-Minute Lesson Model

The following chart suggests a sequence and time requirement for the Lesson 1 procedure.

40-minute class	Instructional Procedure and Student Response: Lesson 1 Target Skill: Cue Words for Comparison
20 minutes	Introduction: Review the concept of cue words by referring to narrative time-and-place cue words. Introduce comparison cue words. Help students construct a class list of words that alert readers to similarities and differences. Students copy list to retain in their writing notebooks.
10 minutes	Show Student Model: Show the students the model provided for this lesson. Have them check it against what they listed. Provide them with a thesaurus for further investigation of cue words.
5 minutes	Students share findings. Store list in writing notebooks.

Lesson 2: Using Cue Words in a Comparison Paragraph

a) Model how to construct a comparison paragraph of several sentences using cue words. For this model use the data from the CraftPlus Comparison Analysis Organizer you and the class created in Chapter 3. Select the one you feel is the most appropriate for your students.

Use many cue words in your paragraph model—the object in models and in practice writing is to overdo the Target Skill, without being concerned about graceful writing. After you create this model, keep it in your writing instruction notebook to be used in future lessons.

Alternatively, you may have a student volunteer do the modeling from the CraftPlus Comparison Analysis Organizer she prepared in the Chapter 3 lesson. Prepare her organizer as an overhead transparency prior to the lesson. Ask the volunteering student to read the organizer entries to the class. Then, in an interactive class-writing activity, have her construct a paragraph from that sample, using cue words in sentences contributed by the class, and guided by you. Remind students to keep related information together.

Rebekah compared apartments using the CraftPlus Comparison Analysis Organizer and then wrote a paragraph using cue words (see Reproducibles #26 and 27).

If you used **Optional Lesson B** in Chapter 3 to show students how to use a flipbook to make comparisons, you will find a corresponding Optional Lesson—about writing a comparison paragraph with cue words using entries from a flipbook—on page 40.

b) Following your modeling of how to use cue words to write a comparison paragraph, ask your students to retrieve the CraftPlus Comparison Analysis Organizer they completed in Lesson 2 of Chapter 3. Have them write a comparison paragraph using those organizers as their source of attributes.

In these first attempts, do not require them to follow the conventional presentation of similarities first. But after several practice sessions (which might include homework journals), have them go back and revise their practice paragraphs to follow a consistent format (see Lesson 3).

Sample Forty-Minute Lesson Model

The following chart suggests a sequence and time requirement for the Lesson 2 procedure.

40-minute class	Instructional Procedure and Student Response: Lesson 2 Target Skill: Using Cue Words in a Comparison Paragraph
15-20 minutes	Introduction: Model writing a comparison paragraph using as many cue words as you can. Use either the flipbook or the CraftPlus Comparison Analysis Organizer as the source of comparisons by multiple attributes. Alternative: A student volunteers to model; class helps the volunteer compose the paragraph; you guide.
15-20 minutes	Students try it out: Students write a comparison paragraph using cue words. Use either the flipbook or the CraftPlus Comparison Analysis Organizer for source of comparisons by multiple attributes.
5 minutes	Students share their writing with a partner: Students save paragraphs in their writing notebooks.

Student-Writing Models for Lesson 2

Until you have collected samples from your own students, you can use the following student responses to this lesson as models for your instruction. (📄 See also Reproducibles #28 and 29.)

Maria

Like sprite, Water is edible and a liquid.

Both Sprite and water have a clear color.

Sprite and water are made out of different things.

Unlike Sprite, water has a bland taste.

Both maps show the capitals and the states. Also They are the same size. But one map is a political map and the other map is a feature map. Unlike map 1 Map 2 has a boorder. Map 1 Shows a compass but map 2 doesn't. Although both maps have their similaritys and diffrences, theyre still both very educational and will help you Learn.

High School
Jan. "05

Lesson 3: Conventional Comparison Paragraph Text Structure (Organization)

Writers, by convention, usually deal with similarities first when they compose a comparison paragraph. Please note that this convention is not written in stone—writers are free to do pretty much what they want, constrained only by their readers' need for clarity and interest.

📄 a) Model the conventional presentation format by reading aloud one of the following samples paragraphs. Provide students with copies of this text (see Reproducible #30) so that they can read along with you.

As they and you read the text aloud (chorally) ask them to identify and mark their copies of the text to show where the author showed similarities and differences. (Use markers or sticky notes.) Guide them to point out that similarities come first, followed by differences.

Models of the Conventional Format

Example for Grades 4-6 (Comparing Horses and Zebras):

> **Both** horses and zebras are herd animals and grass eaters. They are **similar** in that they are hoofed mammals. **Like** a horse, a zebra's young are called foals. They are also **alike** in that they have a mane and tail. **But whereas** a horse's mane is long enough to flop over and hang down its neck, the zebra's mane is short and stands straight up from its neck. Their tails are also **different**, with the horse's made up of longish hairs entirely and the zebra's shorter with a tuft of longish hair just at the end.

Example for Grades 7 and Higher (Comparing Memoir with Autobiography):

> Memoir (personal narrative) and autobiography are **similar** in that they relate events in the life of the writer. **Both** genres are presented in the first person singular and usually in the past tense. In **both**, writers make liberal use of what William Zinsser (1987) calls "inventing the truth," for it is impossible for most of us to remember every detail of a past event, setting, or the other persons involved. Nor can we usually remember conversations verbatim. What **sets** memoir **apart from** autobiography is its focus on a number of vivid or intense episodes, rather than describing a chronological series of events over a lifetime.

b) Have students write a comparison paragraph, using one of their saved organizers. Ask them not only to use cue words, but also to construct their paragraphs in the conventional format of **similarities first followed by differences.**

Ask students to share their paragraphs with peer partners and check each other's work for cue words and format. Remind them to save their written pieces in their writing notebooks.

Lesson 4: Exception to the Conventional Format—Each Attribute Compared in Turn

Writers are not compelled to follow convention. But they are compelled to be consistent. For example, a writer may choose to treat similarities and differences on an attribute-by-attribute basis.

📄 Model this alternative attribute-by-attribute organization by reading the sample Horse and Zebra comparison paragraph given here. Provide students with copies of the text so that they can read along with you. You will find a copy of this text in Reproducible #31.

a) Oral exercise: Have your students read the text with you. Ask them to identify and mark their copies of the text to show where the author addresses each attribute. Point out that the author discusses both similarities and differences per attribute. (I have identified the attributes in parentheses.)

<u>Model of the Attribute-by-Attribute Format</u>

Horses and zebras are fast moving animals that inhabit grasslands (*movement*). They are **both** grazing animals (*eating mode*). They have sharp front teeth to crop grass and large flat teeth for grinding it (*teeth types*). Horses can be found all the continents with grasslands **but** zebras occur in the wild only in Africa (*geographical distribution*). As grazing animals, they depend on their fleetness of foot to avoid predators (*defenses*). Additionally, they depend on their hooves for defense. Their hooves are solid and sharp edged (*hoof type*). The zebra's hooves are narrower than a horse's but are equally lethal.

(This writer has first addressed the attribute of eating habit and its relationship to habitat, discussing similarities and differences in horses and zebras vis-à-vis that attribute. Then she addresses the attribute defense and its relationship to hooves, showing similarities and differences in hooves.)

b) Writing: Have students write a comparison paragraph using one of their saved organizers. Ask them to not only use cue words, but also to construct the paragraph in the alternative format of showing the similarities and differences as they address each attribute in turn.

Ask students to share their paragraphs with peer partners and check each other's work for cue words and format. Remind them to save their written pieces in their writing notebooks.

Developing writer's (grade 6) response to Lesson 4.

Gabrielle
Grade 6

Crocodiles and Alligators

Like an alligator, a crocodile is a cold-blooded animal. As you propoly know cold-blood means there body tempature changes to the things around them. Both alligator, and crocodile, live in tropical rainforests were there is a creek where they can swim.

Crocodiles and alligators both have a diffrent shape mouth. As you ~~probably know~~ the crocodile has a V shape mouth and the alligator has a U shape mouth. Unlike a crocodile the alligator is a much faster reptile.

> ## Optional Lessons

Optional Lesson A: Using a Flipbook Organizer

The comparative attribute-analysis of ducks and chicks, created as a flipbook in Optional Lesson B in Chapter 3 (see page 31), is followed by a model comparison paragraph constructed from it.

Attributes	Statements
Voice	Ducks quack; chickens cluck.
Water	Ducks swim; chickens don't.
Mouths	Ducks have bills; chicks have beaks.
Class of animal	Ducks are birds; chicks are too.
Reproduction	Ducks lay eggs; chickens do too.
Covering	Ducks have feathers; chickens do too.
Feet	Ducks have webbed feet; chickens have separate toes.
Eat	Ducks eat fish, insects, plants, and seeds; chickens mainly eat insects and seeds.

> **Both** ducks and chickens are birds and lay eggs. Ducks, **like** chickens, have two legs and feathers. They are **similar** in that they are **both** vegetarians. **But**, ducks have **different** kinds of beaks and feet. Their beaks, also known as bills, are flat and rounded **while** chickens' are pointy. A duck's feet are webbed, **unlike** a chicken's, which have separated toes. Ducks like to swim, **and** chickens don't. **Unlike** ducks, chickens eat a more limited diet.

a) Model this ducks and chickens paragraph by writing it slowly on an overhead transparency or on the board, saying each sentence aloud before you write it. As you compose, point out to your students how you have chosen to use the conventional approach of showing similarities first, followed by differences. Also note that you have kept related attributes together (*mouths* and *feet* are *physical traits*, and *swimming* and *eating* are *behavioral traits*).

Call their attention to each comparative cue word (they're bolded in the sample paragraph) by emphasizing it orally as you write it, and by circling or otherwise highlighting it.

b) Now ask the students to retrieve one of the flipbooks that they created previously, and ask them to write a comparison paragraph about their pair, using their reference list of cue words.

Students should keep these practice paragraphs in their writing notebooks. They can also practice this craft skill in homework writing journals. Remind them that the Target Skill is using cue words in a comparison paragraph to let the reader know what the relationship between bits of information is.

Optional Lesson B: Contrast Text Structure

When writers deal only with differences, the paragraph text structure is called *contrast*. This text structure uses comparison cue word vocabulary that deals solely with differences, words and phrases such as *in contrast, not, unlike, dissimilar*, etc.

> Regular flowers have petals that are shaped alike. These flowers have radial symmetry. Tulips and daisies are examples of regular flowers. **In contrast**, the petals of irregular flowers have different shapes and the flowers **do not have** radial symmetry. Orchids and snapdragons are examples of irregular flowers.

Single Contrast-Structure Sentence

As always, when you teach your students to write contrast-structure paragraphs, you will move from the simple to the complex. Begin by showing them how to write a single **sentence** that uses a pair of opposites. You can integrate lessons about antonyms with this lesson about writing sentences of contrast.

a) Help students brainstorm a list of attribute antonyms or opposites. (These will mostly be adjectives and adverbs). Examples: *inside* and *outside*, *up* and *down*, *over* and *under*, *hot* and *cold*, *graceful* and *clumsy*.

b) Model for them how you'd construct a sentence from one of the pairs of antonyms. (Prior to the lesson construct your model of a sentence using a pair of antonyms. Record it in your lesson notes.) Then ask the students to select a pair from the list and construct a sentence on their own.

Sample model: (little and big) *How can one little dog give us so many big problems?*
You can do this exercise in any content area. A math list of opposites, for example, might look something like this: add and subtract, multiply and divide, positive and negative, rational and irrational, greater than and less than, equal and unequal.

Models of Contrast Sentences:

a) A positive number is **more than** one while a negative number is **less than** one.

b) When you **multiply** a positive number by a proper fraction, the answer is always **less than** the number, but when you **divide** a positive number by a proper fraction, the answer is always **greater than** the number.

c) Some solutions are **acidic** and some are **basic.**

d) Mammals are **warm blooded,** but reptiles are **cold blooded.**

e) Longitude lines run **vertically** on maps, whereas latitude lines run **horizontally**.

Have your students list pairs of antonyms from as many content areas as they can. Then ask them to work in partner pairs to create single **sentences** using those antonyms. Share the results with the class.

Contrast-Structure Paragraph

After students get the idea with single sentences, you can move on to writing a contrast-structure paragraph. Do not, at this point, demand graceful writing: this is **practice on a specific Target Skill!**

Your model: Prior to the lesson, construct a paragraph using a pair of antonyms. Record it in your lesson template.

Sample model:

> On Friday nights I like to go to bed early so I can get up early. But my friend Joe prefers to stay up late on Friday nights then sleep in late the next morning. I'm an early bird and he's a night person. It would be tough for us to room together in school.

Optional Lesson C: Combining and Extending Sentences with Cue Words

Comparative cue words often do double duty. They can help extend sentences to provide variety in form, length, and rhythm that keeps readers from falling asleep. Without such variety, falling asleep is exactly what Gary Provost (in his succinct work, *100 Ways to Improve Your Writing*, 1985) warns us our readers will do. He illustrates with the two following paragraphs standing in contrast.

> *"This sentence has five words. Here are five more. Five-word sentences are fine. But several together are monotonous. Listen to what is happening. The writing is getting boring. The sound of it drones. It's like a stuck record. The ear demands some variety.*
>
> *Now listen. I vary the sentence length, and I create music. Music. The writing sings. It has a pleasant rhythm, a lilt, a harmony. I use short sentences. And I use sentences of medium length. And sometimes, when I am certain the reader is rested, I will engage him with a*

sentence of considerable length, a sentence that burns with energy and builds with all the impetus of a crescendo, the roll of the drums, the crash of the cymbals—sounds that say, listen to this, it is important."

Illustrate sentence variation with models of sentences extended and varied by comparative cue words, then have your students try some themselves.

Sentence-Variation Models

Series of Short and Simple Sentences

A chicken is a bird. A duck is a bird. They lay eggs. A chicken clucks. A duck quacks.

Using cue words that extend and relate sentences:

Both *ducks and chickens are birds. They* **both** *lay eggs.* **Unlike** *chickens, ducks don't cluck, they quack.*

Series of simple sentences

Maps are flat. Globes have curved surfaces. Maps and globes show latitude and longitude.

Using cue words to extend and relate sentences:

While *maps are flat and globes are round, they* **both** *show latitude and longitude.*

Provide your students with paragraphs of short, simple sentences on a topic of interest to them. You might extract the paragraphs from elementary-grade-level informational books that use short sentences.

Have your students practice combining and extending these sentences, using their comparison-cue-word vocabulary list during the practice.

Models for Optional Lesson C: Short-Sentenced Paragraphs

1. Some school field trips can be interesting. A trip to an aquarium might be ok. Sharks and whales are worth seeing. A trip to a zoo is pretty boring. We have seen all the animals before. There is nothing new there. Zoo trips are for little kids. Big kids are not interested in zoo animals.

2. Lunch is always a problem. You get sick of pizza and hamburgers. Our cafeteria has good pizza. Sometimes you just want something else. Salads might be nice. So would ribs. And yogurt, either regular or frozen. The food is supposed to be healthy. Salad is a healthy food. So is yogurt.

Make sure your students appreciate how cue words, aside from their basic relationship-defining function, are a powerful tool for changing sentence form and length to keep their writing from being deadly dull. This craft skill will be increasingly useful in their writing as its length and complexity grows. (Sentence variation is one of the major criteria in most state-writing-assessment rubrics.) Provide your students with ample opportunity to practice using cue words (transitions) as a sentence-variation technique

> Assessment

The assessment criteria for the descriptive piece students write at the end of the genre block are the Target Skills you have taught and your students have practiced during this instructional period. Your objective is to evaluate how well (using a numerical or letter scale) they are able to use the specific skills.

Sample Assessment Rubric (See other examples in Appendix 1):

Comparison Paragraph—Target-Skill Application	3 Applies skill creatively and competently	2 Applies skill competently	1 Attempts to apply skill	Not scoreable
Identifies attributes of the things compared.				
Uses comparison cue words.				
Presents text in a consistent format (similarities then differences or attribute by attribute).				

> Remember

- Cue words help readers understand the relationship of one fact or idea to another.

- Cue words help writers extend and vary sentence structure to add grace and style to their writing.

- Using cue words within paragraphs helps prepare students for the more difficult task of inter-paragraph transitions that they will face in high school and college writing courses.

CHAPTER 5
Step 4: Organizing and Writing a Comparison Paper

⟩ How Writers Organize a Comparison Paper

Writers organize a comparison paper in the same way they organize any other multi-paragraph expository piece: by clumping or grouping related facts and ideas together. (The exception is describing a process and giving directions, which are written as a sequence of steps.)

The lesson sequence of this chapter first takes students through organizing a simple multi-paragraph informational piece. This provides a solid review of the principle of clumping related facts or ideas together. Subsequent lessons show students how to convert the clumps to paragraphs and then link them to compose a comparison paper.

⟩ The Comparison-Paper Genre Block

This fourth step in the instructional sequence is a genre block. At the end of the block, students will write a comparison paper for assessment.

During the instructional period your students will

       a. clump attributes and name the rationale of their clumping

       b. order the clumps in a logical fashion

       c. write a comparison paragraph about each clump

       d. write a multi-paragraph comparison paper with a beginning and an end for assessment

All state and local writing standards or grade-level expectations call for students to write specific genre pieces with a beginning, middle, and end. The instructional sequence and genre blocks of this book focus on the middle, that is, the craft skills directly associated with the comparison genre. You will find lessons about beginnings and endings in **Optional Lessons** starting on page 54.

> A well-designed writing education program necessarily includes instruction in general (non genre-specific) writing-craft skills, such as beginning techniques (both hooks and introductory paragraphs) and ending techniques. If your incoming students do not have these general craft skills, the best time to teach them is at the start of the year. You can teach beginning and ending techniques outside of genre blocks, or you could add those lessons to the "description" genre block.

The genre block sample provided here is based on a fourteen-day schedule. It includes time to review beginning and ending techniques with your students. Without that review, the sample genre block would take twelve days. Finally, you can extend the block by adding days devoted to practice in sorting attributes and logically ordering paragraphs.

Day 1	*Lesson 1: Clumping Related Information*	Use the table of contents of a non-fiction book to show students the clumping of related information. Model listing and sorting, articulating the rationale of your groupings. Students make lists and sort information into clumps.
Day 2	*Lesson 1 (cont)* Students complete sorting, then share what they did. *Lesson 2: Ordering the Groups (Paragraphs)*	Model ordering. Students order their groupings. **Homework Journals**—List, sort, name rationale for the groupings.
Day 3	*Genre Paper: Prewriting*	Students select a pair to compare for their genre-block paper. They begin identifying multiple attributes and filling in a graphic organizer. Conduct conferences with students to help them identify attributes.
Day 4	*Lesson 3: Sorting Attributes, Naming Rational for Groups, and Ordering Groups*	Model sorting attributes from duck-and-chicken analysis or one created in Lesson 2, Chapter 3 (see page 28). Students state rationales for grouping, create a legend, and order the clumps. **Journals returned**.
Day 5	*Lesson 3 (cont)*	Complete the sorting, stating rationale for grouping and ordering the clumps. Students continue the prewriting of their genre piece for the remaining time.
Day 6	*Practice skills from Lesson 3*	Students sort, name rationale for, and order groups from one of the Comparison Analysis Organizers they created in Lesson 2, Chapter 3. Conduct conferences to help students sort and state rationale for groupings.
Day 7	*Genre Paper: Prewriting*	Students continue attribute analysis, clumping, naming, and ordering clumps for the topic pairs they selected for their genre papers. Continue conferences to provide guidance.
Day 8	*Lesson 4: Writing the Paragraphs*	Model how to compose paragraphs from the ordered groups from the model in Lesson 3. As you compose, invite students to suggest sentences using cue words. Students start the drafts of their genre papers.
Day 9	*Writing Workshop*	Students work on their genre papers, completing prewriting and drafting paragraphs. Continue conferences to provide guidance.

Day 10	*Lesson 5: Review Beginnings*	Model a variety of hooks. Students try some out as a Target Skill, writing about pictures. **OR** *Writing Workshop: Students Drafting, Conferencing, or Revising Genre Papers—* Conference and provide guidance.
Day 11	*Lesson 6: Introductory Paragraphs*	Model a variety of introductory paragraphs. Students identify introductory paragraph functions in non-fiction text sources. **OR** *Writing Workshop:* Review of class standards of writing conventions; Students editing their genre papers.
Day 12	*Lesson 7: Endings*	Model a variety of endings. Students try some out on the picture-prompted piece they wrote to try hooks. **OR Genre papers due.**
Day 13	*Writing Workshop*	Students complete genre papers—adding beginnings, introductory paragraphs, endings. **OR Review** of class standards for writing conventions. Students edit genre papers.
Day 14	*Evaluation Piece*	Genre papers due at end of period.

> The Lessons

Lesson 1: Clumping Related Information—Organizing a Simple Informational Expository Piece

a) Show students the table of contents of an informational book either by using a Big Book borrowed from a primary grade teacher or by projecting a table of contents from a simple informational book. Discuss what the headings in the table of contents represent (they represent related information). Leaf through the Big Book or the book from which you took the table of contents and read bits of information under the various headings from the contents table to show that the text information matches the heading or chapter title. Remind students that all expository writing is organized by clumping (sorting) related information or ideas into paragraphs or larger sections.

b) Now ask students to select a subject that they feel they know quite a bit about and ask them to make a list of words or phrases (bits of information) they associate with that topic. Tell them that as a model you will do the same, selecting a topic appropriate to your grade.

Construct your list on the board or on a projected overhead slide, but actually have it prepared and recorded in your lesson template prior to the lesson.

c) Model sorting and naming the rationale of groupings: When you and your students have completed your lists (ten to twenty items are useful) go through the thought process you would use to sort your model list of words or information facts into clumps of related material. Use geometric shapes, colors, or letters to designate the groups. Emphasize that is helpful to state the rationale for the grouping as you form the clumps, and apply an appropriate label to each group.

Example: If your list of words/facts/information were about a school project, your thought process might then sound like this:

This item is about cost so it belongs with these others which are all about the economics of the project. And these two things are about places. Ooh, and here's something else about location. I'll put them all together in a group called location. This item seems to be about availability. Do I have something else here about availability? Yes, here are two more. What's this? Oh, yes, that's the material about people in the project. I will call that clump personnel. I need to investigate that further and get more information. OK, I can see there are going to be at least four major sections to this report: economics, availability, location, and personnel. Hmmm, this one doesn't seem to fit with anything else, I'll just put it aside for the moment.

d) Now have the students sort their lists of topic facts or phases into clumps of related information and use geometric shapes, colors, or letters to designate their various groups. Remind them to state the rationale for each grouping they create. Circulate around the room, helping them with their sorting.

Sample Forty-Minute Lesson Model

The following chart suggests a lesson sequence and the time requirement for the Lesson 1 procedure.

40-minute class	Instructional Procedure and Student Response: Lesson 1 Target Skill: Clumping Related Information
10 minutes	Model: Introduce the concept of clumping related information by discussing tables of content of simple informational text and reading from various headings.
10-15 minutes	Teacher and Students all make a list of words associated with a topic about which they have a good deal of knowledge.
10 minutes	Model: Sort the items on your list, articulating your thoughts as you do so. Use geometric shapes, colors, or letters to designate groups. Emphasize stating the rationale of the sorting/naming of each group.
5-10 minutes	Students: Start to sort and name the groups of their own listed items. They will continue this the next day in class.

Novice writer's (grade 4) response to Lesson 1.

Lauren   Practice

                                        list linkin k

                    Justin Timberlake

◊ N'sync   △ Tearin'up my Heart
○ Basketball   △ Merry christmas,
□ Tennessee   Happy Holidays
□ blue eyes   □ 18 years old
◊ pop music   ○ Shaq O'neal
◊ costumes   □ He doesn't like his
□ curly   curly hair
□ curly, Bounce   △ Cd
△ Here we go   ◊ concert, Orlando

Student-Writing Model for Lesson 1

📄 Until you have collected samples from your students, use Reproducible #32, the student response shown at the bottom of page 48, as a model for your instruction.

Lesson 2: Ordering Groups of Related Information

After writers have grouped related information, they will need to tentatively order the groups (or clumps), in essence creating a presentation outline. This outline, of course, is subject to change as the writer works his way through drafts of the piece. Frequently he will go off in a different direction than he originally planned. This is good. Remind your students that "writing is thinking" and that a writer's thoughts will inevitably evolve as he writes his way through a piece. In fact, this connection between the drafting process and the thought process offers one of the major satisfactions in writing, to say nothing of its value to effective expository writing.

> If you require your students to turn in an outline before they begin writing their draft (always a questionable requirement), allow them full latitude to modify their outline as they write. This includes their taking a whole different approach to the piece.

a) Number your groups (paragraphs), demonstrating for your students how you plan to order them in your model piece. You might point out that writers usually go from the general to the specific. Example: If a piece were about whales, the material about what they look like or what a whale is would probably come before how they breathe.

b) Ask the students to put their groups or clumps in a tentative order. Have them explain to a partner the logic of their ordering.

📄 Provide your students with the following handout, How to Organize Any Expository Paper (Reproducible #33). Students should keep their copies in their writing notebooks.

How to Organize any Expository Paper (except process description or giving directions)

- Gather lots of information or ideas about your topic. Place each item on individual cards or papers—or make a list.

- Sort the cards or items on the list into groups or clumps of related facts or ideas.

- Write down the rationale for your clumping; for example: *These items are all about X.*

- Create a tentative outline by ordering your clumps. Notice what your paper is really beginning to be about.

- Write a draft paper in the order you have decided upon.

- Revise your draft as you discover new ways to make the presentation of your ideas clearer and more logical.

- Add a beginning technique (a hook).

- Construct an introductory paragraph that functions to reveal where you are going to take your reader. Note that the best introductory paragraphs are written after the rest of the paper has been completed, when you know what it is you have said and how you have said it.

- Add an ending technique, providing closure for the reader.

> A convenient way—and the most concrete way for students in grades 4-6 to compile and organize attribute clumps for a comparison paper—is to record each of the attributes from the organizer on a separate slip of paper or on a card. They then can place the slips or cards on a large flat surface and physically sort them into groups.

Lesson 3: Sorting Attributes, Naming Rationale for Groups, and Ordering Groups (Two Class Sessions)

In comparison papers, information clumps (or paragraphs) are composed of related attributes. This lesson, about sorting attributes, is conducted over two class sessions.

a) Give your students a copy of the CraftPlus Comparison Analysis Organizer comparing ducks and chicken by multiple attributes (Reproducible #22). Alternatively, use the organizer you and the class created in Lesson 2 of Chapter 3.

Point out that the *Attributes* column of the organizer is a list. Tell your students they will be sorting the entries in that column just as they would sort the lists they brainstormed for any informational writing.

b) Sorting: Guide your students in sorting the attributes of the organizer into clumps. Using an overhead projection of the Ducks-and-Chickens organizer, you might say something like this: *Here is an analysis of the attributes of ducks and chickens. Let's read the list of the attributes by which we are comparing ducks and chickens. Now we have to solve the puzzle of presentation. That is, in what groupings and in what order should we present this information? All writers must do this after they have collected all the stuff they want to write about.*

Ask students to look at the duck-and-chicken attributes and decide which ones go together. To get them started, do a first grouping as a class and record it on the projected organizer, using a geometric shape or a color mark.

c) Now ask them to complete the sorting using different color marks or geometric shapes to indicate on their individual organizers which of the other attributes they will clump together. Allow them to discuss which attributes go together or what further attributes they might add to the organizer. For instance: They might discuss whether they should put *mouths* with *color* or with the *habitat-and-eating group*? The logic of the clumping is up to the individual writer.

d) Articulating the rationale for the clumps or groupings: After students have completed their attribute clumping, ask them to articulate how the attributes in each clump are similar. They should be able to state a rationale for each clump. Show them how to create a legend or key by using differing colors or geometric shapes to designate their various groupings.

For example, if they put *mouth, color, combs, feet,* and *covering* in a group, they can mark each of those attributes with red and then put a red mark in a text box to begin creating a legend (in the margin of the chart or on a sticky note). After the red mark, they might write *physical description*.

Another grouping might be *behavior (swimming, eating, sounds they make)*. Another might be *animal-class characteristics*—that is, attributes that define an animal's class, such as *reproduction by laying eggs, skin covering,* and *vertebrae*. Students may come up with different words or phrases for their groupings, such as *eating habits, what they do,* etc. That is perfectly fine. Each grouping should have its own color mark and a corresponding entry in the legend.

You should create a legend for the projected class version of the chart over the course of the class period as the students are working on their own charts. This will provide them with a model to follow. You will come back to this work later, so save your transparency or computer file. Have students share with their partners what they did, and then have them put their copies in their writing notebooks.

d) Ordering the Clumps: Once students have identified groups of related information in the Ducks-and-Chicken organizer, remind them they will have to decide which two, three, or four clumps to include in their papers, and in what order to present them.

If your students have not had a good deal of exposure to expository text, they may not be aware that writers usually order their information from the general to the specific. Tell them that you would probably select the group of traits that define ducks and chicks as belonging to the same animal class (*birds*), before comparing them according to *habitat* or *commercial use*.

Have your students order their clumps (paragraphs) and number them. They can number the groups in the legends they created. Give them the opportunity to share their tentative order with a partner.

Sample Two-Session Lesson Model

The following chart suggests a sequence and time requirement for the Lesson 3 procedure.

Two 40-minute classes	**Instructional Procedure & Student Response: Lesson 3** (two class sessions) **Target Skills: Sorting Attributes, Naming Rationale, Ordering Groups**
20 minutes	Teacher and Students: In a whole-class experience, show how to sort attributes using Ducks-and-Chickens model or one the class constructed in Chapter 3 lessons. After you have articulated the rationale for the groupings, model creating a legend.
20-30 minutes	Students try it out: Sort attributes on their copies of the Ducks-and-Chickens organizer, name the rationale for each grouping, and create a legend they share with a partner, then save their charts in writing notebooks. Allow for discussions with peers.
20 minutes	Teacher: Model the ordering of clumps, or paragraphs. Students: Order the clumps they created.
10 minutes	Students: Share with peers. Store work in their writing notebooks.

Student-Writing Model for Lesson 3 (Session One)

📄 Until you have collected samples from your students, use the student response at right as a model for your instruction (Reproducible #34).

Lesson 3 (cont): Students Sort Attributes in Their Own CraftPlus Comparison Analysis Organizers

a) For practice in sorting, group-naming rationales, creating a legend, and ordering of clumps, have your students select one of the CraftPlus Comparison Analysis Organizers they created in the Chapter 3, Lesson 2. Ask

Sorting Duck and Chicken Attributes

1 Class of animal
 Vertabrae
 Covering
 Reproduction — young and egg size

2 mouths
 covering
 colors
 comb   } Description
 wattle under beak
 feet

3 Habitat — water
          ` eat
4. Unique characteristics - voice
                          ` flight

Eighth-grader sorted attributes, stated rationale, and ordered the groups.

them to read through the attribute list they constructed for the pair they analyzed. Encourage them (and make sure they have time) to add more attributes and information.

> Fifth graders in Sarasota, Florida were identifying attributes to compare horses and zebras. A debate arose: could zebras be domesticated and trained like horses? One student claimed to have seen a zebra in a circus act. Another responded that it was probably a horse they had painted with stripes. A web search began. The answer was that indeed a zebra had been trained for a circus act. Learning this, the fifth graders changed the information in their analysis organizer.

b) Next, have your students sort their lists by clumping related attributes. (Students can use cards to physically sort their lists, or they can mark the items on their lists with colors, shapes, or letters.) If a student has too few attributes to sort, help him add more attributes to his organizer. You may also need to help some students with the sorting process. Remind students that as they decide on a clump they must be able to tell why the attributes belong together. Have them create a legend for their groupings.

Following the sorting and group naming have your students share what they did with other students. They should save their work in their writing notebooks.

Further Practice:

At first, students are likely to have a difficult time articulating the rationale for their groupings. It is an abstract skill, and even adults can have a difficult time finding the right word to describe the groupings. Your students will need lots of practice to master this skill. (This is why it is necessary to teach writing comparison each school year. The craft remains the same, but as students' vocabularies and life experiences grow, the application of the craft is refined.)

Students will profit from your showing them many examples of filled-in organizers and guiding them in sorting and describing groups of attributes.

A seventh grader compared two cars in two pictures, sorted each list of attributes, and explained rationale in a legend.

Name Kevin _____ (Grade 7) Date 04/29/04 Period 7th

Item #1: Car #1   Item #2: Car #2

♡ light blue
♡ four wheels (white)
○ windows
○ license plat
○ lights
✱ hoods up
○ wind sheild wipers
✱ trunk's open
○ hub caps
☆ brand new
○ doors
✱ instyle

♡ four tires (black)
♡ spare tire (black)
♡ blue car
☆ old fashion
○ stirring wheel.
○ two seats
○ pedals
○/thin tires
○/doors

♡ = Color
☆ = Age
○ = special Features
✱ = location

Student-Writing Model for Lesson 3 (Session Two)

📄 Kevin's car comparison (at left) is also available as Reproducible #35.

Lesson 4: Writing the Paragraphs

a) Tell your students, "Now we need to write a paragraph about each clump of related attributes." (Remind them of the Chapter 4 lessons about writing comparison paragraphs using cue words.)

Model, on chart paper or an overhead projection, how to compose a paragraph for each of the two, three, or four attribute groupings the class came up with in Lesson 3 (see page 50).

As you model, invite students to compose and suggest sentences, referring as they do so to the list of comparison cue words. Depending on the writing experience of your students, you may show them how they can also add supporting details they know (such as numbers, authoritative quotes, graphics, descriptive details) to enlarge on the information. (See *Building a Writing Community* and *Listen to This: Developing an Ear for Expository* for lessons about supporting details, an important writing skill looked for on state assessment reading and writing test.)

b) When you have completed the comparison paragraphs that make up the middle of the comparison paper, show your students that it is now, after they have written the content of the paper, that they can most effectively create a hook, an introductory paragraph, and an ending technique. If your students have not had writing instruction in beginnings, opening paragraphs, and ending writing-craft techniques, you should insert lessons on those skills at this point. (See Optional Lessons on page 54.)

A seventh grader used a question hook and cue words to compare two photographs of hairdos.

Handwritten student sample:

Name Lourdes
Date 4/23/04 Pd. 4th

◎ Target Skills:
Hook
Cue words

Can hairdos be anymore attention-catching? Hairdo #1 is a really good model to wear to prom or a wedding. However, the second hairdo is more extroverted and colorful. Not many people would wear it and only daring people are able to get it.
Both hairdos are ideal to make a big impression and get you noticed. Hairdo #1 has curls and braids involved rather than spikes like hairdo #2. The shape of the first hairdo is more round whereas the second hairdo is columnar. Hairdo #2 looks heavy as compared to the first hairdo that looks lighter.

Lesson 4 (cont): Students Write Their Own Papers

After you have modeled how to write the paragraphs of a comparison paper based on the Ducks-and-Chickens model, have your students begin drafting their multi-paragraph genre papers. Remind them to use the Comparison Cue Word reference sheet as they construct their paragraphs (Reproducible #25).

Students may write their papers paragraph-by-paragraph over one to several days. Encourage them to change the paragraph order during the drafting process if they feel a different order would make more sense, and to add supporting details. When the content of the paper is written, ask them to complete their papers with a hook, an opening paragraph, and an ending technique.

Bear in mind that the Target Skills for this exercise are *organizing* (sorting, group-naming rationales, and ordering clumps) and *drafting a multi-paragraph comparison piece*. The demonstration of these skills is the primary objective of the assessment. The assessment rubric for the comparison paper additionally contains the criteria of beginning and ending, and writing conventions (as do all genre block rubrics).

Editing: Allow a full writing period for students to edit their papers. (If they also do some minor revising, all the better, but it is not required.) At the start of this class period, briefly review with your students the grade-level expectations for writing conventions. Remind them that writing conventions of *capitalization*, *punctuation*, and *spelling* are criteria for the genre block rubric.

📄 Rebekah's assessment paper is available as Reproducible #36. Remember, your students' writing may not be graceful at this point. What they have produced will qualify as a first draft.

> Optional Lessons

The following lessons review writing-craft techniques for composing beginnings and endings, general craft skills that are necessary for writing in all genres. If your students' knowledge of and facility with these craft skills is insufficient, you will want to extend the comparison-paper genre block to include instruction and review in the skills they need. Otherwise, regardless of how well they have mastered comparison skills, readers will find their comparison papers incomplete and unsatisfactory.

Optional Lesson A: Beginnings—Hooks or Leads

The beginning of every written piece should engage or "hook" the reader. A hook should be easy to read, attract attention, and introduce the topic. A hook rarely includes the main ideas. The hook (or lead) may consist of a single sentence or several. The main function of the hook is to encourage the reader to keep reading.

Some common non-fiction (personal narrative and expository) categories of hooks:

- question
- contrast
- anecdote
- play on words
- amazing or startling fact
- definition
- quotation
- hyperbole

Students can and should construct, or add to, the above list by analyzing non-fiction literature. Excellent models of hooks and their application can be found in *Ranger Rick*, *Odyssey*, and *Scientific American* magazines. Select the magazine most appropriate for your students' reading levels. Magazines and newspapers in general provide good examples of beginning and ending techniques. If your students gather a great number of first sentence hooks, with your help they can sort them into categories like the ones in the list provided here.

Show your students examples of as many of different kinds of hooks as you can find in magazines and other non-fiction materials. Have them try out some of these leads as Target Skills in short written pieces about pictures they select from the class collection. Remind them that the hook has to mention or be related to the topic.

Here are some examples of how hooks can be applied to a comparison paper. Model them for your class.

Question: Are ducks and chickens related? You might think so when you take a close look at the two species.

Definition: A duck is pretty much a chicken that can swim. Or so I thought until I studied them more closely.

Contrast: The Artic tundra and the equatorial rain forests are degrees apart in latitude and temperature. Yet if you study them closely you will find they are close in a many ways.

Anecdote: When I was young I used to think a brook and a creek were pretty much the same thing. I heard people in my town call the fishing places around us Branch Brook and Carson's Creek. It was confusing.

Have your students try some different hook techniques in order to find one that best fits their papers. You can leave it at that; in other words, just requiring a hook for the first genre paper. Later, you can review introductory paragraphs and add that as a Target Skill in your second comparison-paper genre block.

A novice writer's (grade 8) response to Lesson A.

> Hooks- Question, sound words, exclamation, setting
>
> Zinnnng. Your reel goes off the drags, going crazy.
>
> Do you like river fishing? Well I do.

Optional Lesson B: Function of the Introductory Paragraph

Once students have mastered an assortment of age-appropriate hooks, we need to show them how to write introductory paragraphs. As with hooks, an introduction is often (and probably best) written after a piece is drafted. Because the function of the introductory paragraph is to tell the reader where the writer has gone with the topic, the writer needs to have gone there first. And, as observed earlier, writers often don't know exactly where they were going until they have gotten there.

The content of a piece and the author's purpose determines the function of the first paragraph. It may be one to several sentences long. In the introductory paragraph, a writer may

- give background information

- tell how he got interested in the subject

- tell how she felt about the subject

- tell why the topic is important to the reader

- establish the reason for comparing the subjects of the paper

Teach how to write an introductory paragraph in the same fashion as you do all craft lessons:

a) Model examples of introductory paragraphs in magazine and newspaper articles or use the essays in *Listen to This* (see Bibliography).

b) Discuss the skill: Ask students, "Which approach might be appropriate for an introductory paragraph for an essay about bicycle helmets and safety in which you detail an accident you had without a helmet? Which might you use for an article about kidney dialysis or origami, subjects with which your readers may have no familiarity? Which might you select for a piece about a favorite hobby of yours? Which one might be a good one for a comparison paper about lacrosse and hockey?"

c) Have students try it out: Provide your students with magazines that are two or three grades below their reading level. *Ranger Rick, Junior National Geographic*, and such are great ones for this exercise. Have students select and silently read an article that appeals to them. Have several volunteers read aloud to the class what they think is the introductory paragraph in the article they have chosen. Ask them to identify what function the paragraphs seem to perform. Ask all your students to try to identify the function of the introductory paragraphs in their articles. Allow for peer discussion.

d) Show student models:

Developing writer's (grade 7) response to Lesson B.

Name Ryan

Date 4/27/04   Pd. 4th

Grade 7

🎯 Target Skills:
Hook
Intro paragraph
Cue words

Everyone come to the car show from the classics to the new concept cars! Cars have always been something I loved. I found out from the comparison I made with the cars how much technology in cars have increased from the era of 1910's-1920's to the era of 1950's-1960's.

e) Provide for students' practice: Have students practice creating a hook and introductory paragraph for one of the practice pieces they wrote during the description genre block, or one of the pieces they wrote in their journals to practice other Target Skills. When they write their introduction, ask them to identify its function.

f) Model again: how you might use some of the introductory functions in a comparison paper. The following two paragraphs are examples of introductory functions for a comparison papers about birds. Construct others for your lessons, choosing subjects about which you are knowledgeable or passionate. Record them in your lesson templates.

> **The reason for comparing the things (following a question hook)**
> *Thinking of raising ducks or chicken for a living? You might take a closer look at the two fowls and see which one fits your farm environment and market prospects.* (The body of this comparison paper focused on the attributes of the two birds in regard to commercial production; eggs, life of birds, feed requirements, and such.)

How the author feels about the subject (following a talk-directly-to-the-reader hook)
If you're a bird watcher like me, you learn to tell birds apart by looking carefully at all their features. It is so amazing to discover the tiny things that distinguish one bird from another. You feel almost like a detective. The various warblers are the toughest to distinguish so you have to really tune in to all the clues. (The body of this comparison paper focused on the similarity and differences between palm and pine warblers.)

Application: Lastly, have your students select an introductory-paragraph type to use in the multi-paragraph comparison piece they have been writing in the current comparison paper genre block.

Grades 4-5 Instructional Hint

Please note that the task of writing an introductory paragraph will be quite difficult for fourth or fifth graders who may still be a novice writers. Do not expect their introductory paragraphs to be more than a sentence or two. Some will repetitively pick the same function because it is the only one they understand and are comfortable with.

As students gain experience, they will enlarge their repertoires of hook techniques and introductory functions.

Optional Lesson C: Endings

Readers need a sense of closure, a satisfying ending that informs them that the piece has come to a finish. A good ending technique leaves the reader thinking, *That was interesting,* or *I enjoyed that.* Student writers need to know that simply putting *THE END* at the bottom of a piece is ineffective and lame. They must be taught effective ending techniques.

Ending techniques come in as large a variety as those for beginnings. The best way to find them is the same way we did for beginnings: that is, by finding examples of what professional writers do and then categorizing them. Some techniques writers commonly use to end non-fiction pieces are

- telling or restating how they feel about the subject

- inviting the reader to learn more and referencing where

- circling back to the hook and using the same device or style

- quoting the key person in the piece

- drawing an analogy or a conclusion from the ideas or examples in the piece

- reiterating the main points (in a paper of five pages or longer)

Teach how to use ending techniques in the same fashion as you did beginning techniques:

a) Show examples of ending paragraphs in magazine and newspaper articles or in mentor texts such as the essays in *Listen to This* (see Bibliography.) Project the provided list of ending techniques for all to see. Have your students copy the list or give every student a copy to start.

b) Discuss the skill. Ask students to identify the ending techniques in samples of easy non-fiction texts.

c) Students identify techniques in texts: Again, use magazines such as *Ranger Rick* and *Junior National Geographic* for this exercise. Have your students select and silently read the endings of articles they choose. Ask them to write the ending paragraphs they found on an index card. In groups of four, have each student read the paragraph she chose and then ask the group to identify the function it performs. If students identify new or different techniques have them add the techniques to their lists (saved, as usual, in their writing notebooks).

Have the students note that few professional writers begin their ending paragraphs with "'In conclusion…"

📄 **d) Model several ending techniques** for the class, using short models you have prepared ahead of time and kept in your writing instruction notebook. Also show your class student sample models of this skill. (See Reproducible #37.)

e) Students try it out: Students apply some of the ending techniques to practice pieces they have saved in their writing notebooks or in their pieces in their writing journals.

f) Application: Lastly, have them select a technique to use in the multi-paragraph piece they have been writing in the current comparison paper genre block.

<u>Grades 4-5 Instructional Hint</u>

Fourth and fifth graders may end their pieces with one sentence based on the techniques listed in the chart. Students in later grades can be shown how to extend these ending techniques to a paragraph of several sentences.

Optional Lesson D: Using Additive Transitions (Grades 6 and Up)

Until your students have mastered the skill of organizing and writing comparison pieces, do not introduce them to the relatively advanced skill of using additive cue words to move their readers smoothly from one paragraph to another.

When you think they are ready for this skill, here are some of the early additive cue words you'll want to introduce

- and
- along with
- for one thing
- additionally

- also
- for instance
- again
- nor

- or
- besides
- another

Teach these cue words in the same fashion you introduced comparison transitions. That is, first show students how to use the words within a paragraph (sentence-to-sentence transitions). After the students have practiced and mastered that, show them how to use the same cue words to make the transition from one paragraph to the next.

Example: Additive transitions *within* a paragraph

> All sports do not all demand the same skills. **For instance**, marathoning doesn't require the coordination that basketball does. **And** ping-pong doesn't require the muscle strength of wrestling.

Example: Additive transitions *between* paragraphs

> All sports do not all demand the same skills. **For instance**, marathoning doesn't require the coordination that basketball does. **And** ping-pong doesn't require the muscle strength of wrestling.
>
> **Nor** do all sports demand the same oxygen-processing capacity. A marathon is an aerobic event with a huge demand for oxygen and the processing of lactic acid. **On the other hand**, sprinting 60 meters is largely an anaerobic event. Oxygen processing is at a minimum for sprinting.

Notice how the basic concepts and skills of comparison underlie these paragraphs. Without those skills, the additive cue words would be of little or no value. That is why students need to master the use of comparison cue words and organizing multi-paragraph comparison papers before we introduce them to additive transitions, the use of which will make their writing considerably more graceful and fluent.

> Assessment

The assessment criteria for the descriptive piece students write at the end of the genre block are the Target Skills you have taught and your students have practiced during this instructional period. Your objective is to evaluate how well (using a numerical or letter scale) they are able to use the specific skills.

Sample Assessment Rubric (See other examples in Appendix 1):

Comparison Paper—Target-Skill Application	3 Applies skill creatively and competently	2 Applies skill competently	1 Attempts to apply skill	Not scoreable
Pre-writes using a graphic comparison organizer identifying multiple attributes.				
Orders paragraphs logically.				
Uses comparison cue words.				
Uses beginning and ending techniques.				
Uses grade-level capitalization and punctuation conventions.				

> Remember

Writers compose a multi-paragraph comparison paper by first identifying the attributes of the two things to be compared. They compare the two things by these attributes, using a graphic tool, to show similarities and differences. Then they sort these attributes into clumps of related attributes. Next, they order the attribute clumps in a logical progression. They then write paragraphs about each clump, using comparison cue words to help their readers navigate within and between paragraphs. They choose a beginning technique to get their readers into their piece and an ending technique to give the readers a satisfying sense of closure.

Your students need to do these things. When they do, they are writers.

Bibliography

Articles:

Fernandez, Melanie *Reading/writing connection (Opinion Paper). RIESEP,* 1998

Shanahan, T. *Reading-writing relationships, thematic units, inquiry learning…In pursuit of effective integrated literacy instruction.* Reading Teacher, *51:1,* 12-19. (1997)

Tierney, R., Soter, A., O'Flahavan, J., and McGinley, W. (1989). The effects of reading and writing upon thinking critically. *Reading Research Quarterly, 24,* 134-173

Professional Books:

Ackerman, Diane. *A Natural History of the Senses.* New York: Random House, 1990

American Psychological Association. *APA Publication Manual,* (Fourth Edition, eight printing - 1996)

Bryson, Bill. *The Mother Tongue.* New York: William Morrow, 1990

Freeman, Marcia S. *Building a Writing Community,* Gainesville, FL: Maupin House Publishing, 1995

_____*CraftPlus®: A K-5 Writing Program - video-based staff development resource.* Gainesville, FL: Maupin House Publishing, 2003

_____*Listen to This: Developing an Ear for Expository,* Gainesville, FL: Maupin House Publishing, 1997

_____*Models for Teaching Writing-Craft Target Skills,* Gainesville, FL: Maupin House Publishing, 2004

Lakoff, George and Johnson, Mark. *Metaphors We Live By.* Chicago: U of Chicago Press, 1980

Macrone, Michael. *Animologies.* NY: Doubleday, 1995

Marzano, Robert. *What Works in Schools: Translating Research into Action.* Alexandria, VA: ASCD, 2003

Provost, Gary. *100 Ways to Improve Your Writing.* NY: NAL Penguin Inc. New American Library, Mentor Book. 1985

Reeves, Douglas, Ph.D., *Accountability in Action: A Blueprint for Learning Organizations* Denver: Advanced Learning Press, 2000

Bibliography

Professional Books (continued):

Richardson, Laurel. *Writing: a Method of Inquiry, Chapter 32,* in Norman K. Denzin and Yvonna S. Lincoln, editors. *The Handbook of Qualitative Research.*, Sage Publications, 1994

Scholes, Robert. *The Rise and Fall of English.* New Haven, CT: Yale University Press, 1998**,** pg. 96)

Russell Baker, Anne Dillard, Alfred Kazin, Toini Morrison, Lewis Thomas. *Inventing the Truth: the Art and Craft of Memoir.* Boston: Houghton Mifflin Company, 1987 Edited by William Zinsser

Zinsser, William. *Writing to Learn.* NY: Harper & Row, Publishers, 1988

Children's Books: Comparison Structure

Brown, Margaret Wise. *The Important Book.* NY: HarperCollins Publishers, 1949 (Harper Trophy book, ISBN   0-06-443227-0)

Freeman, Marcia S. *A Bird's-eye View.* Chicago, IL: Rand McNally, 1999

Fletcher, Ralph. *Twilight Comes Twice.* NY: Clarion Books. 1997

Johnson, D. B. *Henry Hikes to Fitchburg.* Boston: Houghton Mifflin, 2000

Larkin, Patricia. *Subway Sonata,* Brookfield, CT: Millbrook Press, 2001

MacLachlan, Patricia. *Through Grandpa's Eyes,* NY: Harper and Row Publishers, 1980

Selsam, Millicent E. *Big Tracks, Little Tracks.* NY: HarperCollins Publishers, 1958, 1995

Spier, Peter. *Crash! Bang! Boom!* Garden City, NY: Doubleday and Company. 1972

Wiles, Deborah. *Freedom Summer.* NY: Atheneum Books, 2001

Wood, Audrey. *Quick as a Cricket.* Boston: Houghton Mifflin Co., 1996

APPENDIX 1
CraftPlus® Principles and Practices

The methodology in this book is based on the principles and practices of CraftPlus®, the approach to writing instruction that I developed over many years of teaching students to write and training teachers in instructional strategies. CraftPlus also reflects my own extensive and varied experiences as an author.

The approach is based on explicit instruction in a progressive curriculum of writing-craft skills. Research and field experience has validated that this is the only way to achieve effective writing educational outcomes.

Professor Robert Scholes (1998) puts it this way: "Our [teaching] range, our capabilities go no further than craft. Even in creative writing courses, craft is all that can be taught. " Scholes further asserts that writing instruction should be based on models. "Our aim should be to help students learn how to produce a good, workmanlike job with a written essay whenever they need to. It means mastering the medium through the study of models. Students who are asked to write about anything at all must have a chance to see how that kind of writing is done, and to study both good and bad examples of it."

As Professor Scholes advises, CraftPlus instruction utilizes professional and peer writings to provide students with models of specific Target Skills™ that you select to teach and that your students get to practice and master.

Knowing the principles and practices of CraftPlus will help you use this book most effectively. If you already familiar with CraftPlus, you may wish to read the Quick Review that begins this appendix. If you are new to CraftPlus, you will need to read the detailed treatment of these principles and practices that follows the review. You can learn much more about the instructional concepts and methodologies of CraftPlus, and their classroom application, in *Building a Writing Community: A Practical Guide* and *Listen to This: Developing an Ear for Expository*, and particularly in the *CraftPlus: K-8 School-wide Writing Program and Staff Development Resource*.

> A Quick Review of CraftPlus

Principles

- The writing process is what writers *do*; writing craft is what writers *know*.

- Writing craft is a set of specific skills that encompasses organizational and literary (composing) techniques, and writing conventions.

- Writing must be viewed as an academic subject that is explicitly taught in every grade.

- Effective writing instruction proceeds from the simple to the complex, from the concrete to the abstract.

- CraftPlus emphasizes non-fiction, which is 99% of the writing 99% of us do in our lives.

- CraftPlus links writing to reading by teaching young writers the four strategies that all writers must employ to assure their readers' comprehension. It teaches young writers how to recognize these strategies in their reading, and how to effect them in their writing.

Practices

- Instruction employs specific writing-craft Target Skills™ as a focusing mechanism.

- Writing is taught using models from printed text and student writing.

- Students select the genre or form to which they will apply the Target Skills, when you teach general writing-craft skills. (Most composing and writing convention skills and techniques are general, while most of the organizational skills are genre specific.)

- In grades 2 and above, genre-specific writing-craft skills are taught in instructional periods called *genre blocks*.

- Beginning in kindergarten, writing craft is delivered through a scaffolded, recursive, and progressive curriculum. Each grade contributes to the expansion and development of student writing-craft skills.

- Student classroom writing consists of 85% practice and 15% performance, as is true for instruction in sports, art, music, dance, and all crafts.

- Writing instruction is conducted in a daily writing-workshop environment or in short lessons that the students apply during content area writing.

- Traditional writing-process mechanisms are modified for effective peer response, revision, and editing.

- Revision is emphasized. Target Skill instruction gives students specific revision goals.

- Student writers maintain personal writing notebooks; teachers keep personal writing-instruction notebooks.

- Writing assessment is objective, based on students' application of specific (targeted) craft skills they have been taught and have practiced. Therefore, all students can succeed.

> A Crash Course in CraftPlus

Central to CraftPlus is the concept of Target Skills™-instruction, which I designed in 1986 to focus on the specific writing-craft and writing-process skills that we select to teach our student writers, have them practice, and then ask them to demonstrate through application in their writing.

Target Skills focus your students' learning on specific writing techniques. Target Skills include organizational, composing and revising, or conventions-based writing-craft techniques.

- **Organizational Skills**: sorting and classifying information or ideas for expository text, chronological ordering of events for narrative text, prewriting techniques, beginning and ending techniques, paragraph text structures, transitions, and more

- **Composing and Revising Skills**: specificity, literary devices, supporting detail types, voice techniques, dialog tags, providing clues for inference, and more

- **Conventions**: punctuation, capitalization, parallel construction, grammar, and more

The writing that occurs in response to a Target Skill lesson is practice writing and is not graded. It is, however, evaluated by peers during peer conferences to determine whether the writer has "hit the Target." You do review students' practice writing, for diagnostic purposes and to help you plan further instruction. The important thing is to keep the focus on *learning*: formal assessment comes later.

In fact, student writing should be eighty-five to ninety percent practice and ten to fifteen percent performance. In this respect, writing is no different than other craft endeavors such as music, dance, art, or sports. That is, a great deal of practice of explicitly taught craft skills, with only occasional formal performances to demonstrate the degree of mastery of those skills.

> Methodology

CraftPlus Target Skill lessons are based on the principle of teaching craft through modeling or simulations. Lessons follow this instructional sequence:

- Show students examples of a specific skill or technique in literature (Target Skill lessons about writing-process mechanisms are demonstrated through simulations).

- Discuss with students why writers use the skill or technique—what does it do for the reader?

- Model use of the skill or technique, both orally and in written form.

- Give students a chance to try the skill or technique out—first orally, then written—allowing for approximation.

- Provide opportunities for a good deal of practice in applying the skill, with lots of encouragement and with supplementary modeling and instruction.

- Finally, assess students' mastery of the skill or technique in a required written piece. (See Assessment on page 68.)

Pictures: Writing-Topic Stimulators

To practice writing-craft skills, students need something to write about. Photographs, magazine pictures, personal snapshots, and art prints are all excellent resources for stimulating topic ideas when you ask students to practice the Target Skills you have taught them.

Pictures, as topic stimulators, work so well because they are concrete. That is, students can hold a picture, feel it, see it, and talk about it. Pictures are versatile: a given photo can be used to stimulate writing for many Target Skills. Finally, picture-prompted writing takes advantage of people's dominant learning mode, which is visual.

Perhaps the most important feature of this technique is that students can select pictures that match their background experiences and interests. They know the vocabulary of the topic. They can concentrate on craft and not struggle with content. That is why you should avoid assigning topics when students are practicing a writing technique. The time for assignments is when your main objective is to authentically assess your student's knowledge of the assigned topic though their writing about the topic.

> Chris   strong
>   verbs
>   A boy is sitting criss-cross, apple sauce,
> strumming a guitar. He is fingering a cord.
>
> He is wearing a gray T-shirt and dark
> green shorts.

In every grade, from kindergarten through high school, teachers should introduce pictures in the first week of school as a source of topic or inspiration for writing. To this end, you should have a wide collection of color photographs in your classroom.

Lesson Plans

Teachers who implement CraftPlus develop and maintain a Teacher's Writing Instruction Notebook. It contains genre and Target-Skill lesson plans, genre-block schedules, curriculum documents, assessment rubrics, bibliographies of literature models, examples of collected student work that can serve as further models when lessons are repeated, and other resources they need to teach writing craft.

To record lesson plans, CraftPlus teachers use a template such as the following example. (This sample is from a lesson in Chapter 2: Step 1 – Identifying and Describing Attributes.) The template, which can be used for any Target Skill lesson, helps you prepare, remember, revise, and present your lessons. (See Reproducible #38.)

CraftPlus® LESSON PLAN TEMPLATE

Objective (Target Skill): Identifying attributes of maps

Genres to which the skill can be applied: Description, comparison

Time parameters: During first two weeks of fall term—Lesson takes two forty-minute sessions. Reinforce through homework journals.

Materials: 28 copies total, of three or four different maps.

Literature Model Sources: Atlases, a large map (map projected by overhead transparency), my own model of a paragraph describing the class map.

Procedure

Session One: Students look over maps and construct a class chart of attributes of maps from background knowledge and my teaching. I help them articulate the attributes that might include several examples (example: different colors may represent *political subdivisions* which is the attribute)

Then students list the attributes specific to their own maps, share information with peers, and store in their notebooks.

Session Two: I model a paragraph describing the class map (or the large map I used yesterday.) I tell students, as I model the paragraph, that I am placing sentences of information about related attributes in close proximity. Students write a paragraph comparing their maps. Share with peer and store in notebooks.

Attached: Two samples of student work in response to the lesson—one novice and one advanced.

Note that CraftPlus lessons are not scripted. It is important that you bring your own style, creativity, and personality to the lessons. The sample teacher dialogues in this book are only suggestive.

Writing-Classroom Sessions and Lessons

A lesson may take place over one or two consecutive forty-minute writing periods. The following charts suggest sequence and time requirements for the **procedure component** of two lessons from this book (Lesson 1 from Chapter 4 and Lesson 3 from Chapter 2).

A one-writing-period lesson sequence

40-minute class	Instructional Procedure and Student Response: Lesson 1 Target Skill: Cue Words for Comparison
20 minutes	Introduction: Review the concept of cue words by referring to narrative time-and-place cue words. Introduce comparison cue words. Help students construct a class list of words that alert readers to similarities and differences. Students copy list to retain in their writing notebooks.
10-15 minutes	Show Student Model: Show the students the model provided for this lesson. Have them check it against what they listed. Provide them with a Thesaurus for further investigation of cue words.
5 minutes	Students share findings and store list in their writing notebooks.

A two-writing-period lesson sequence

40-minute class	Instructional Procedure and Student Response: Lesson 3 Target Skill: Identifying Attributes of Maps
15-20 minutes	Session 1—Introduction to map attributes: Give out copies of several different maps. Allow 5 minutes for students to look over their maps. Tell them the object of the lesson is to construct a class chart of map attributes. Guide them to form a list comparable to the list of map attributes provided in this chapter. (You can give them an abbreviated version to serve as a "seed list.")
15-20 minutes	Students try it out: Have the students list the attributes specific to their own maps.
5 minutes	Share: Have students read their list to a partner and put it in their writing notebook.

40-minute class	Instructional Procedure and Student Response: Lesson 3 (cont) Target Skill: Identifying Attributes of Maps
10-15 minutes	Session 2—Review of map attributes: Give out copies of the class-generated Map Attribute list. Ask for volunteers to read the list. Ask for any additions. Model how to write a paragraph describing the attributes of the projected map or class map. As you model the paragraph, tell your students that you are placing sentences about related attributes in close proximity.
15-20 minutes	Students try it out: Have your students write single-paragraph descriptions of their maps, referring to as many attributes in their text as they can. Do not expect graceful writing, the object of this lesson is to identify and name map attributes.
10 minutes	Share: Have students read their paragraphs to two other students. Circulate to hear the results yourself. Ask peer responders to put a color mark as a compliment for each attribute the writer identified as he described his map. Have students save their lists, maps, and paragraphs in their writing notebook.

Models

The best way to teach writing is through modeling. Models provide students with concrete examples of the applied Target Skill. You can take your models from literature, from student writing, or you can compose models yourself.

Models taken from literature need to be short and easy to read. Luana Mitten, author and national literacy consultant, points out that it is particularly important for teachers to use models that match the length of their students' current writing output. Book-length works are too long to be useful, but short excerpts from anthology pieces can work.

Student writing provides one of the most powerful models for your lessons. Students learning a Target Skill need to see how peer writers handled the same skill. Your students will say to themselves, "Oh, that's what it is supposed to look like," or, "If that kid can do it, so can I!"

When your students write in response to a lesson, ask them to print. Collect two samples of student writing from each lesson, one average and one excellent. With the student-writer's permission, turn these pieces into overhead transparencies (darken the writing where necessary) and keep it with that lesson plan in your writing instruction notebook.

Caution: Never use student work as models of poor work. Create the poor-example models yourself, or ask students to create them on purpose. In fact, you will find that deliberately writing poorly is an effective learning mechanism. Having your students write pieces that intentionally miss the target can actually increase their understanding of a craft skill. Plus, they usually enjoy doing it.

Collecting Models

Debbie Abshire (classroom teacher, writing educator, and national consultant from Sarasota, FL) labels manila envelopes, each with one of the Target Skills under study. She asks her students, as they read independently, to be on the lookout for the writing-craft skills they are learning. Whenever they find examples, they record the title of the piece (usually a book or magazine article), the author, the craft skill, and some of the pages where they observed the skill in use. They then put the information in the appropriate envelope. In this way, Debbie has accumulated a useful bibliography of potential models for her writing-craft lessons.

Genre Blocks

A genre block is a period of time you devote to instruction in a specific genre. During that period, you provide time for your students to develop a piece in that genre. (Pieces can be a paragraph or a complete paper.) The block may last several days or several weeks, depending on how many lessons you present and how long your students can sustain a written piece. For instruction during the block, you select a set of Target Skills needed to support the genre and that are appropriate to your students' background knowledge and writing experience. (See chapters 2-5 of this book for samples of genre-block schedules.)

Over the course of a genre block, students usually take a genre piece of a self-selected topic through the entire writing process. On some days, you present lessons and your students respond by trying to apply the skills or practicing them. On other days, you work with groups of students for review or to help individual students as they write their genre pieces. During the process you support students with brief conferences and revision lessons. Devote the last day or two of a block to writing conventions and editing so students can prepare their pieces for assessment.

Assess the final genre pieces for the application of the Target Skills that you have taught and that the students have practiced during the block. Ask that students keep the practice writing they did in response to the Target Skill lessons (usually a paragraph or so) in their Student Writing Notebooks for use during future revision and editing lessons.

<u>Selecting Target Skills for a Genre Block Piece</u>

The Target Skills you select should **usually** consist of

- One **organization** technique or scheme specific to the genre.

- One to three **composing** skills that can be used in the genre.

- One writing **convention** (capitalization, punctuation, grammar, etc.).

Most students in grades 4 and higher can handle several Target Skills during a given block. Of those Target Skills only one or two should be a new skill or technique.

NOTE: In the three genre blocks described in the instructional steps of this book, writing conventions were not selected as one of the genre Target Skills. But, just as you can extend the instructional period with lessons from the Optional Lessons provided for each step, you can extend it also by including a writing convention Target Skill as one of the criteria for the genre piece and by conducting lessons in the use of that convention.

> Assessment

Under the classic assign-and-assess approach to writing education, assessment is predominantly a **subjective** exercise. But by teaching specific writing craft using the Target Skill concept, you turn writing assessment into an **objective** exercise. All your students, not just the naturally gifted writers, have the opportunity to succeed.

Rubrics

You can make up a rubric for any given piece using the application of the Target Skills as the criterion. Superior levels of grace and sophistication can be awarded with bonus points above those earned by simply "hitting the target." (You may change the language of the criteria to suit yourself or your students, or eliminate the language and just use numbers or letters.)

You can use your state's assessment rubric when your instruction for the piece has addressed the criteria of that rubric.

An example of a single Target Skill assessment rubric:

Applies Target Skill creatively.	3
Applies Target Skill competently.	2
Attempts to apply Target Skill.	1
Makes no attempt to apply Target Skill.	Not scoreable

An example of rubric assessing multiple Target Skills:

Comparison Paragraph— Target-Skill Application	3 Applies skill creatively and competently	2 Applies skill competently	1 Attempts to apply skill	Not scoreable
Identifies attributes of the things compared.				
Uses comparison cue words.				
Presents text in a consistent format (similarities then differences or attribute by attribute).				

Further Assessment Means

You can assess writing achievement in many ways when instruction is writing-craft specific. Some other ways to assess student progress are

- quizzes (As a subject matter, writing craft can be assessed just like content knowledge in any subject area.)

- student writing notebooks and their upkeep

- practice pieces (Students select one or more from their journals or lesson responses, edit them, and submit them for evaluation.)

- participation during lessons

Ungraded practice writing should account for about 85-90% of the writing students do in school. Formal assessment is done only on the final genre-block pieces in which students are expected to demonstrate the writing-craft skills they have been taught and have practiced.

> Remember

CraftPlus principles are consistent with contemporary educational theory and best practices. Its instruction is explicit and presented through models. It moves from the simple to the complex, and from the concrete to the abstract. It supports risk-free practice of writing skills followed by authentic and objective assessment.

CraftPlus follows a progressive curriculum of grade-appropriate writing-craft skills. And, that curriculum emphasizes non-fiction writing, which accounts for 99% of the writing we do in our lives.

CraftPlus instruction ties writing to reading by making developing writers aware of the choices authors make and the impact those choices have on their readers.

APPENDIX 2
Literary Devices

› Comparison as a Descriptive Technique

Writers use simile and metaphor to create imagery. *She's as wily as a fox. Drivers exited the road like ants abandoning an anthill. The essay assignment was an albatross around his neck.* Or, they use other phrases that help reader form comparative pictures in their minds. *The hurdlers remind me of gazelles.* Obviously, these devices and phrases will only work if they speak to the reader's background knowledge. The following chart details the variety of literary comparisons I have compiled with students over the course of my writing-education career.

Single-Attribute Literary Comparisons
(Presented in approximate order of difficulty and instructional level.)

- -er or -est: comparatives and superlatives

  The teacher plays the best music while we march.   (text from a first grader)

- like:

  Alex runs like a cheetah.   (text from a first grader)

- just like:

  When you go in that room, it feels just like a library.   (text from a fourth grader)

- simile: as _____ as _____.

  Ophelia was as crazy as a coot.   (text from a eleventh grader)

- it reminds me of:

  The lake reminds me of the pond behind my uncle's house.
  They have the same pebbly edge.   (text from a fifth grader)

- the same as _____ except (but)

  Spaghetti is the same as macaroni except it's longer.   (text from a sixth grader)

- so _____ that

  My dog is so big that his feet hang over the front seat when he rides in the car.   (text from a third grader)

- metaphor: saying that one thing is another to show how the two share an important attribute

  Six T-shirted gazelles soared over the hurdles and raced to the finish line. (text from a high school student)

> Simile and Metaphor

Similes are more concrete than metaphors. They draw a direct comparison from one thing to another. Similes identify the shared attribute for the reader. For example: *Her face was as red as a beet. They followed maniacally, like lemmings leaping into the sea.*

In metaphor, the reader has to make the comparative connection and infer the shared attribute, which may be an abstract one. For example, *The kid is a pit bull.* The reader has to deduce that the kid and the dog share the attribute of *ferocious tenacity.*

Professional writers of both non-fiction and fiction use simile and metaphor as colorful ways to describe an attribute of a person, thing, or action. They also employ these literary devices to relate the new and unfamiliar to the known and familiar. They are telling us, "Don't panic, this new stuff is a lot like something you already know." In both applications the device causes the reader to get more involved with the text.

The following passages show how useful simile and metaphor can be when you are trying to create imagery.

Simile from *James and the Giant Peach* by Roald Dahl

> "So what would you call it if you saw a grasshopper as large as a dog? As large as a large dog. You could hardly call that an insect, could you?"

Metaphors from *Twilight Comes Twice* by Ralph Fletcher

> "… dawn drinks up night's leftover darkness, the great black pools and deep-rooted shadows." "With invisible arms dawn erases the starts from the blackboard of night."

Metaphors from *Life With Mother* by Russell Baker

> *"When you are the only pea in the pod, your parents are likely to get you confused with the Hope Diamond."*

Lesson for Teaching Simile

Using the picture-prompt and writing-craft lesson model as described in Appendix 1, you can teach your students how to construct both conventional similes *(as…as)* and ones using the word *like* to compare two things by a physical or sensory attribute. These are the easiest literary comparisons to construct: *as small as a pebble, as loud as a junior high band, like a bull in a china shop, like a kid in a candy store.* The attribute lists from Chapter 2 (Reproducibles #2-9) will be a useful reference for students to have in hand.

Procedure: Read a children's book that contains many similes to your students. *Quick as a Cricket* by Audrey Wood is everyone's favorite model text for this lesson. Point out the similes you read the book. Next, have students select an attribute such as color, then select a specific color, such as yellow, then think of two things that are yellow. Ask them to compose a simile likening one thing to another: *The dandelion is as yellow as the sun.* Invite them to try different attributes. *It smells like licorice. The dog's hair feels like steel wool.* Have them share their compositions with each other.

Have them identify and collect similes from their independent reading and contribute them to a class list. Publish the list as a reference for them to add to their writing notebooks.

Lesson for Teaching Metaphor (Grades 5 and Above)

The easiest way to teach metaphor is to begin with an attribute and something that epitomizes that attribute. For example, *messy*, and the epitome of messiness, *a pigpen*. Now name a new thing that might share the same attribute. For examples, a room could be messy. Thus the metaphor, *This room is a pigpen*. Point out the difference between the metaphor (the attribute is not revealed by the author—the reader has to deduce it) and the same thought in the form of a simile, *This room is as messy as a pigpen*.

Construct a three-column chart like the following for your lesson. Provide several empty rows and ask students to make up examples or find examples in their independent reading to enter in the chart.

Attribute	Epitome of the attribute	Another thing sharing that attribute	The metaphor
messy	pigpen	my room	My room is a pigpen.
handsome	Adonis	a man	He is an Adonis.
unique	the Hope Diamond	child	Your parents are likely to get you confused with the Hope Diamond.

> Remember

Good readers visualize as they read. Therefore, good writers should strive to create imagery for their readers. Conventional similes and metaphors as well as the other comparing techniques discussed in this appendix document are the tools writers need to do that.

APPENDIX 3
Comparing Texts

Writing to compare texts is no different than writing to compare any other entities. Identifying **attributes** is the first step, followed by analyzing the text for multiple attributes using a modified Venn diagram, employing comparison cue words to write comparison paragraphs, and organizing a multi-paragraph paper. Make text attributes the focus of lessons during Step 1 (Chapter 2) of the instructional sequence for crafting comparison papers.

Students may need, in English classes or on state tests, to compare texts of different **genres**. They need to be familiar with a large variety of genres and be able to recognize them by their **defining attributes**.

The study of text attributes is easily incorporated into reading instruction to reinforce the concept. Literature analysis should not only address content issues such as motives or themes but also consider the characteristics of the genre, and especially, the **writing craft** the author used to make the literature noteworthy.

> Attributes

Text attributes fall into three categories:

- **Physical features**: art illustrations, charts, close-ups, cross sections, text density, diagram, font size, font styles, glossary, graphs, headings, illustrations, index, insets, labeled photographs, lists, maps, paragraph length, photos, schedules, table of contents, tables

- **Genre-specific attributes**: purpose, content, veracity of information, text structure, arguments, characters, setting, plot, motive, theme, transitions

- **Writing-craft attributes**: anecdotes, ending techniques, hooks, onomatopoeia, metaphor, irony, anadiplosis, synecdoche, repetition, quotations, specificity, strong verbs, dialog tags, voice

> Attribute Lists

The following text attribute lists are presented in reproducible charts within this Appendix:

Physical Attributes and Features of Text

Genre Attributes of Fictional Narrative

Genre Attributes Of Non-fiction Narrative

Genre Attributes of Expository

General Writing-Craft Attributes

Writing Craft Specific to Fictional Narrative

Physical Attributes and Features of Text (visual)

Density: number of words per page

Font sizes: estimate the size based on the standard font-size (12) used in word processing documents

Font types: serif (like this) or sans serif (like this)

Font styles: regular, bold

Word length: predominant word length or the range of lengths

Sentence length: predominant length; range of the various lengths

Paragraph length: average number of lines per paragraph

Use of color

Text features or navigational aids to reading informational text: headings, lists, illustrations, maps, tables, graphs, charts, labeled photos, close ups, glossary, index, table of contents

Specific to Narrative:

> **Poetry line meter**: number of syllables per line, pattern

> **Paragraph length**: average number of lines per paragraph

> **Text features**: indented paragraphs, art illustrations, table of chapters, quotation marks, in drama—stage direction in parentheses

Genre Attributes of Fictional Narrative

Sub-genres: adventure, fantasy, historical, mystery, plays, poetry, romance, science fiction, westerns

Purpose: entertain, instruct, or both

Intended audience: everyone, or specific gender, age or interest group

Chronological order of events: time passes, flashbacks may break the overall strict time ordering, but chronological order is maintained within a flashback

Rings true: While fiction is made-up, it is not fake. That is, its psychology and emotions must ring true, even in science fiction or fantasy. The history in historical fiction must be basically accurate or otherwise noted by the author in the preface.

Characters: major and minor: people or animals acting like people (anthropomorphic stories)

Motives: (why the main character acts as he or she does): for attention, to please another, love, revenge, greed, power, political gain

Setting: time, place, mood, and atmosphere

Plot (presented here as problem and resolution):

- Lost and found

- Character solves problem or reaches goal

- Character survives nature

- Good guys defeat bad guys

- Mystery or crime is solved

- Boy meets girl and problem or misunderstanding is resolved

Tension: setbacks, misunderstandings

Irony (a plot device: a situation in which the unexpected, the opposite of what the reader expects happens): Example: *After going to a lot of trouble to get traded to a Texas team in order to spend more time with his family, a player gets a divorce.*

Theme: Examples: hard work pays off, beauty is only skin deep, don't judge a book by its cover, honor is its own reward, honesty is the best policy, goodness triumphs over evil, promises are made to be kept, crime doesn't pay, we value what we earn, the joy of giving is greater than the joy of having something ourselves, look before you leap, he who hesitates is lost, love conquers all, honor is worth defending

A consistent point of view: first person (I saw the team board the bus.) or third person (omniscient observer) The team boarded the bus. main character's perspective throughout, or alternating chapters of two main characters view point

A beginning technique or hook

Plot resolution: and denouement (wrap up of all the loose ends for the reader).

Expository bits included: information, definitions, philosophy, or opinion

Genre Attributes Of Non-Fiction Narrative

Personal narrative, biography, memoir and *autobiography* are akin to fiction, in that they share with fictional narrative chronological organization and subject matter (being about people).

Purpose: to entertain or instruct

Audience: all interested individuals

Organization: chronological; memoir may be organized topically but within the topic chronological order is maintained

Content: people and events

Hooks: The beginning techniques for non-fiction and fiction are different and varied. Refer to the charts of these techniques presented for reproduction in the Appendix.

Beginning: establishes who, where, when, and what

Descriptive details: rich in comparisons, active verbs, specificity, literary devices, etc.

Transitions: related to changes in time, place, action

Endings: While non-fiction narratives are not plotted like fiction, they do contain exciting, tension filled events, conflicts, problems, and setbacks. Personal narrative usually ends with the author revealing strong feeling or reactions to the related event, what he or she learned from that event, or what significance the event played in the author's mental or moral development.

Point of View: first or third person relates the story

Verb tense: usually past tense but also may be in the present tense

Other features: may include minor bits of expository writing within the story or dialogue: definitions, information, philosophical asides, directions, etc.

Crafting Comparison Papers

Genre Attributes of Expository Genres

Sub genres: description, informational text, directions, process description, opinion, review, persuasive argument; schedules, menus, manuals, poetry, business letter

Purpose: inform, explain, illustrate, evaluate, compare, define, persuade

Intended audience: specific (teens, children, retirees, business people, scientists, ranchers, restaurateurs, teachers, principals, etc.) or the general public

Organization: Clumps of related information or ideas; sequence of steps or items; no passage of time (except in supporting narrative vignettes)

- logical order based on natural divisions within the topic
- hierarchy of related ideas based on importance to writer
- sequential order (as in directions and process descriptions)
- alphabetical order
- comparison
- sequence of questions and answers
- problem and solution
- cause and effect
- logical series of arguments

Paragraph Text Structures: description, comparison, contrast, main idea with multiple examples, main idea with supporting details, whole and its parts, sequence, cause and effect, definition, question and answer, problem and solution

Veracity of facts

Verb tense: usually present, with the exception of explanation of a past event (*Why the Pilgrims Came to America*)

A beginning (hook) and **an ending**

Transitions (reflecting organization scheme): addition, comparison, cause and affect, sequence, considering alternatives, referring back, etc.

General Writing-Craft Attributes

Strong verbs: to create imagery.

After slogging through a muddy and grueling three-miles, the cross-county runners found the guts to sprint the last hundred yards. (As opposed to: *After running through a muddy and grueling three-miles, the cross-county runners decided to run faster in the last hundred yards.*)

Verb tense

1. present tense, as in most expository writing: If you think art is important, you are on the right track.

2. past tense, as in most narrative: The next morning he called upon two or three of his friends, who merely confirmed what he had already heard.

Active or passive voice

1. active: ***We call*** *that habitat a wetland.*

2. passive: *This habitat* ***is called*** *a wetland.* (Passive voice raises the question, "By whom?")

Literary devices: to create imagery and engage reader

1. Alliteration: ***Slugs*** *leave a* ***slimy*** *trail.*

2. Onomatopoeia: *He landed in the pond with a big* ***kerplop.***

3. Simile: *I was clinging to my dad's arm* ***as tight as a snail on a fish tank.***

4. Metaphor: *When* ***you are the only pea in the pod***, *you parents* ***might mistake you for the Hope Diamond*** (Russell Baker in *Inventing the Truth*).

5. Personification: attributing human characteristic to animals or things: *The leaves* ***danced*** *across the lawn.*

6. Analogy: showing that one thing is like another: *Pouring money into that broken-down car* ***is like*** *spitting in the ocean.*

7. Antithesis: *How can one* ***small*** *dog give us such* ***big*** *problems?*

8. Hyperbole (extreme exaggeration): *I've told you* ***a thousand times*** *to close the back door when you come in.*

9. Anadiplosis: repeating a word or phrase that ends one phrase or sentence, or paragraph in the next phrase, sentence, or paragraph: *I am really* ***hungry***, ***hungry*** *enough to eat a horse.*

10. Irony/Sarcasm (see *Writing Craft Specific to Fiction* for irony as a plot device): a use of words to signify the opposite of what the words would normally express *"Great job, Lucy!"* (after Lucy has really botched up her assignment).

General Writing-Craft Attributes (continued)

11. Play on words: *Now, **spider silk** crosshairs are **spinning out** of existence.*

12. Synecdoche (using a part to represent the whole): *We can't keep the boys home now that they have **wheels**.*

Specificity: use specific nouns in place of general ones to create imagery and help reader connect text to self. *We ate blueberry pancakes with Vermont maple syrup.* (instead of *We ate breakfast.*)

Imbedded definitions: to engage and save reader a trip to a glossary. *Eagle claws, called talons, help them grip their prey.*

Repetition (repeating for effect):

"We shall go on to the end, we shall fight in France, we shall fight on the seas and oceans, we shall fight with growing confidence and growing strength in the air, we shall defend our Island, whatever the cost may be, we shall fight on the beaches, we shall fight on the landing grounds, we shall fight in the fields and in the streets, we shall fight in the hills; we shall never surrender…" (Sir Winston Churchill, June 4th 1940)

Voice technique: the 'aside' to engage reader.

This raccoon is a good fisherman. He's fast as lightning. You've got to be quick to catch a fish with your hands.

Voice technique: using pronoun YOU or WE to "talk to" or engage the reader

When you spend a day at the beach or get a chest X-ray, you are exposed to low-level radiation. (As opposed to: *Spending a day at the beach or getting a chest X-ray exposes a person to low-level radiation.*)

Sentence variation: length and form, to engage reader.

simple: *I have a book.*

compound: *I have a book and I must return it to the library today.*

extended with clauses and phrases:

> ***In the morning** I will take my book back to the library* (participle phrase to start).

> ***Opening the door** and sidling in, Kerry tried to look inconspicuous* (gerund phrase to start).

Purpose: entertain, instruct, persuade, compare, evaluate

Intended audience: everyone, or specific gender, age or interest group

Writing Craft Specific to Fictional Narrative

Using dialogue and description to reveal character: what a character says or others say about him, thinks, does, looks like; character traits include physical, personality, moral, and emotional.

Using dialogue tags to provide for the reader's visualization. Ex: *"You're off the team,"* **yelled Coach Finch**, *pointing to the track gate.*

Establishing characters' motives: (why the main character acts as he or she does): for attention, to please another, love, revenge, greed, power, political gain

Establishing plot and developing it through description of events and dialogue.

Creating tension:

> a. Time pressure from the forces of nature
>
> b. Time pressure from human-imposed deadlines
>
> c. Reader is let in on a fact or secret the character doesn't know
>
> d. Anticipation of a major scene (foreshadowing)
>
> e. Setbacks of injury, weather, losses, mistakes, misunderstanding, and mishaps.

Irony (as a Plot Device): a situation in which the unexpected, the opposite of what the reader expects happens: *After going to a lot of trouble to get traded to a Texas team in order to spend more time with his family, a player gets a divorce.*

Establishing and developing a theme: Theme examples: hard work pays off, beauty is only skin deep, don't judge a book by its cover, honor is its own reward, honesty is the best policy, goodness triumphs over evil, promises are made to be kept, crime doesn't pay, we value what we earn, the joy of giving is greater than the joy of having something ourselves, look before you leap, he who hesitates is lost, love conquers all, honor is worth defending

Using a consistent point of view: first person (*I saw the team board the bus*) or third person (omniscient observer) *The team boarded the bus.* (main character's perspective throughout, or alternating chapters of two main characters view point)

Writing Craft Specific to Fictional Narrative (cont.)

Creating a hook: using a beginning technique:

 a. The author introduces the main character by name.

 b. The main character, named, is thinking or doing something.

 c. The author describes the setting place.

 d. The author establishes the setting time.

 e. The author sets up a conflict or problem in the first paragraph or several paragraphs.

 f. A character is talking.

 g. An event is in progress.

 h. A letter or note.

 i. A prologue describes an event that sets up the story.

Resolving the plot: loose ends are wrapped up for the reader (the denouement).

Adding expository bits: to convey information, give definitions, share your philosophy or opinions on subjects, etc.

APPENDIX 4

Reproducibles

Target-Skill Application	3 Applies skill creatively and competently	2 Applies skill competently	1 Attempts to apply skill	Not scoreable

Sample List of General Physical Attributes
and Associated Vocabulary

NOTE: This list includes attributes that can be quantified by measurement or judgment to be more descriptively precise.

movement or **action**: gliding, slithering, flapping, explosive; *comparative*—faster, more frenzied

number: *specific* (through measurement)—fourteen, a thousand; *non-specific*—many, some, several; *comparative*—more than, fewer, as many as a baseball team

size: *specific* (through measurement)—nine-by-twelve inches, one-hundred yards; *non specific*—large, huge, tiny; *comparative*—larger, as big as

color: purple, green, pale yellow; *comparative*—reddish, sea green

shape: round, oval, cubic, square, columnar, tubular, triangular; *comparative*—box-like, pie shaped

texture: smooth, rough, bumpy, lumpy, soft, fuzzy, slippery; *comparative*—stickier, slickest

special features: written, knobbed, patterned, ribbed, buttoned, zipped

location: under, over, behind, beside, far away; *comparative*—closer, farther away

direction: left, right, up, down, backward, forward

temperature: *specific* (through measurement)—forty-six degrees, three below zero; *non-specific*—broiling, freezing; *comparative*—hotter than, coldest

weight: *specific* (through measurement)—ten pounds, seven grams; *non-specific*—heavy, light; *comparative*—as heavy as, the lightest

age: *specific* (through measurement)—five years old, eighteen months old; *nonspecific*—old, new, ancient, antique; *comparative*—older than the hills

smell: smoky, putrid, floral, acrid, burnt, sweet; *comparative*—like smoke, like burned rubber

taste: sweet, salty, acidic; *comparative*—like licorice, fruitier

sound: *specific*—bass, treble; *non-specific*—loud, soft, grating; *comparative*—high-pitched, low-pitched, raspy, whistling, humming, melodic

state: liquid, solid, gas

symmetry: horizontal, vertical, radial

habitat: underground, den, water, ocean, desert, forest, tundra

orientation: horizontal, vertical, parallel, perpendicular

composition: wooden, metal, plastic, cloth, glass, concrete, cardboard, paper

Sample List of People or Character Traits

physical or **behavioral**: aggressive, agile, boisterous, bookish, calm, clumsy, confused, dignified, energetic, fearless, foolhardy, fragile, fussy, gregarious, handy, hardy, headstrong, illiterate, insane, lazy, likable, literate, mealy mouthed, polite, poor, powerful, punctual, reclusive, relaxed, rude, sarcastic, serene, shy, stingy, sturdy, tall, thin, timid, unkind, verbose, vulnerable, weak, weary

emotional: afraid, angry, annoyed, anxious, ashamed, cheerful, confident, content, creative, delighted, depressed, down, elated, excited, frustrated, furious, glad, guilty, happy, hateful, helpless, hostile, hurt, insecure, irate, irritated, jealous, joyful, lonely, melancholy, morose, optimistic, pessimistic, proud, sad, satisfied, scared, thankful, unhappy

moral or **ethical**: calculating, conceited, cowardly, deceitful, dishonest, faithful, false, honest, honorable, generous, loyal, reliable, trustworthy, sneaky, steadfast, untrustworthy, wishy-washy

Sample List of Science Attributes
(Properties of Matter and Material)

appearance: physical attributes (*see above*)

state: liquid, solid, gaseous

plasticity: brittle, stretchy, bendy, rigid, pliable, flexible

hardness: as hard as a diamond, slate-like, malleable

density (weight per volume): comparative—denser than balsa wood, as light as aluminum, thicker than oil

buoyancy: floats like a cork, sinks like lead

conductivity: resistance, as conductive as copper, insulated

viscosity (liquids—as compared to a standard): flows faster than molasses, as thick as oil, runny like water, gooey as glycerin

miscibility: dissolved in oil, water, glycerin, alcohol, layered like oil on water

reactivity: oxidized, corroded, rusty, etched by acid, inert

Sample List of Botany Attributes

leaf edging: lobed, serrate (like saw teeth), smooth

leaf surface texture: hirsute (hairy), glabrous (smooth, shiny)

leaf and bud position: opposite, alternate, whirled

venation: pinnate (like a feather), palmate (like a hand)

stem: scaly, smooth, hirsute, sticky

fruit type: drupe, berry, pod, capsule, samara, nut

flowers: regular, irregular; solitary, compound, composite, in clusters, in catkins, in panicles, in umbels, in spikes, in heads

sepals and petals: inferior, superior

Sample List of Animal Attributes

features: antennae, beak, bill, ears, feathers, four–legged, fur, invertebrate, microscopic, pileated, pupate, scales, segmented, shell, spotted, striped, thorax, toes, tongue, two-legged, vertebrate, whiskered, winged

behavior: arboreal, aquatic, carnivorous, cold-blooded, domesticated feral, ferocious, herbivorous, insectivorous, larval, omnivorous, predatory, solitary, warm-blooded, wild

Sample List of Map Attributes

physical features: borders, compass rose, contour lines, elevation, grid lines, latitude, longitude, legend, projection, scale, sea level, symbols, topography

land forms denoted: mesa, valley, river, dam, lake, mountain, outcropping, plain, plateaus, mountain range, swamp, bay, coastal flood plain, peninsula, delta

political features and subdivisions: boundaries, state capitals, major cities, counties, township, population

Sample List of Text Attributes

features: art illustrations, charts, close-ups, cross sections, text density, diagram, font size, font styles, glossary, graphs, headings, illustrations, index, insets, labeled photographs, lists, maps, paragraph length, photos, schedules, table of contents, tables

genre attributes: purpose, content, text structure, arguments, characters, setting, plot, motive, theme, transitions

writing-craft attributes: anecdotes, ending techniques, hooks, onomatopoeia, metaphor, irony, anadiplosis, synecdoche, repetition, quotations, specificity, strong verbs, dialog tags, voice

Sample List of Math Attributes

geometric: parallel, perpendicular, conical, triangular, oval, rhombic, rectangular, cylindrical, round, square, two dimensional, three dimensional, solid, plane, oblong, perimeter, area, volume, closed, connected, bounded, concave, convex, regular, symmetrical

numerical: negative, positive, integer, numerals, fractional, real, rational, irrational, whole, part, proper fractions, improper fractions, few, many, some, thousands, a google

algebraic: equality, inequality, variables, quadratic, sets, greater than, less than

measurement: *weight*—heavy, light, scaled, pounds, ton; *length*—long, short, inches, centimeter, meter; *capacity*—full, empty, milliliters, cups, gallons, liter, milliliter

1.) Discriptive attributes
2.) opener onomonapeia
3.) closer universal_yard
4. caps

2/2/04

Beep! Beep! That's the sound of scutteing and hard working media senter workers. Checking out and in books. The media senter has dazzling lights like electric time on the roof when you enter it. In the back it has royal purple on the walls. The books are varyos sizes and shapes. Like 3 inches to 6 inches. Most of them are rectangular and have at least one line of symmetry. The media has at least 1,000 books. Some of the books are old and torn and some are smooth or bumpy. Every body loves the libary at Gulf Gate.

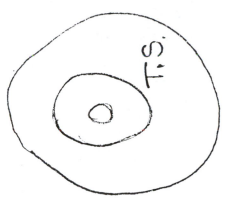

color

texture

His cool, scaly skin is beaded with water. The clear, iridescent droplets shimmer on his lime green scales. His olive green beady eye stares at me. Each of his oval scales is outlined in silver and are smooth to the touch.

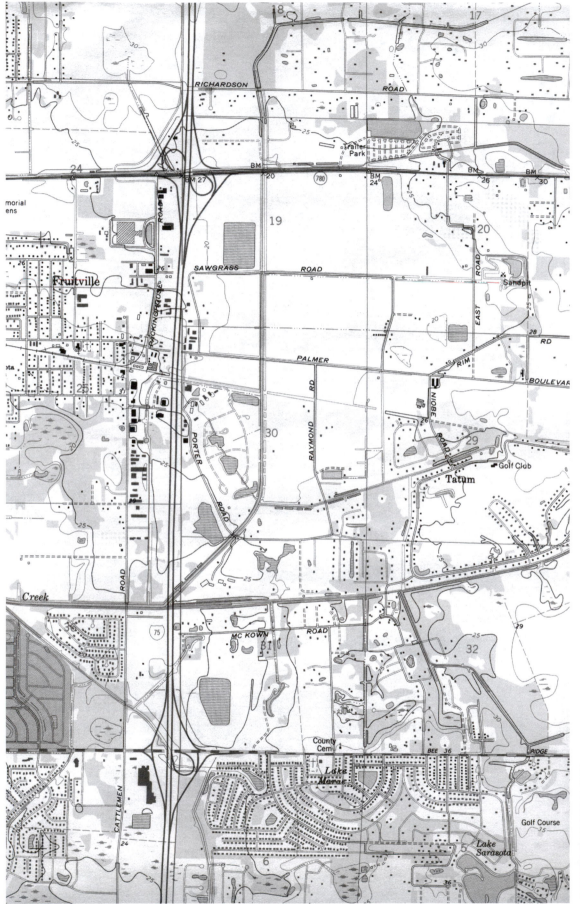

Chris

Map Attributes ◎

red roads
purple lines for highways
small purple squares for houses
blue for lakes and ponds
green for wild land
little blue lines for swamps
(↓ ↓)

· broken black lines for roads that
are going to be built

Alecia

My map has a mileage scale and a compass rose, in the lower right hand corner. It shows the states in different colors with black borders. The map has state names and their capitals and shows some mountains and rivers.

High School!

Some Ordered Presentation Formats

People: physical attributes first then emotional or vice versa, faces before the rest of the person, action before physical features

Setting: from one element in the scene to another; from left to right; from top to bottom; from the central figure out; from foreground to background

Events: chronological order

• •

Emotion the Character Displayed, then Physical Attributes:

Hattie smirked and her high cheekbones jutted up toward her eyes. Her skin was dark brown like her mother's and looked smooth under the yellow streetlights.

(from *Last Summer with Maizon*, Jacqueline Woodson,1990)

Top to Bottom:

All rain forests grow in layers. The top layer, the canopy, is the roof of the forest. It consists of the tops of trees. The understory is beneath that. This part of the forest is made up of palms, short trees, and other plants. The forest floor is the bottom layer. The plants here are not thick because they get very little sunlight.

From One Element to Another:

Addie knew instantly that the big easy chair across from the sofa was Uncle Henry's. His pipe and glasses sat on a small table beside it, and a newspaper was folded on the floor. The old oak rocker, which had been in Grams family for many years, had been brought down from the farm. It reminded Addie of all the times she had rocked on Gram's lap. The rocker stood now near the big window with Gram's knitting basket close beside it on the floor.

(from *Oonawassee Summer*, Melissa Forney, 2000)

Chronological Order of Events:

She baited her hook with a big, juicy worm. She pulled the fishing line away from the polished pole between the reel and the first loop. The line unwound smoothly and silently from her new reel. She flicked the baited book back and forth, swishing it in a big arc over her head. She was ready at last. She swung the hook out over the pool beneath the bridge.

(from *Catfish and Spaghetti*, by Marcia S. Freeman, 1998)

Three Bedroom / Two Bathroom / 1,380 Square Feet

Bath

Closet

Bedroom
12' x 12'

Linen

Utility
Room

WD

Bath

Pantry

Closet

Bedroom
12' x 12'

Kitchen

Dining Area
12' x 12'

Living Area
12' x 24'

Closet

Linen Closet

Bath

Walk-in Closet

Dressing Area

Bedroom
12' x 14'

REPRODUCIBLE #17

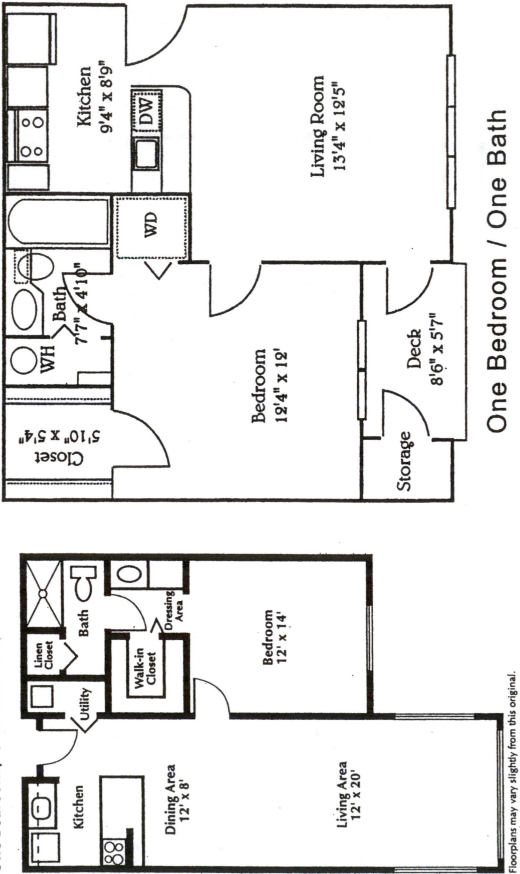

One Bedroom / One Bath

Kitchen
9'4" x 8'9"

Living Room
13'4" x 12'5"

Bath
7'7" x 4'10"

WH

WD

DW

Bedroom
12'4" x 12'

Closet
5'10" x 5'4"

Storage

Deck
8'6" x 5'7"

One Bedroom / One Bathroom

Kitchen

Dining Area
12' x 8'

Living Area
12' x 20'

Linen Closet

Utility

Bath

Walk-in Closet

Dressing Area

Bedroom
12' x 14'

REPRODUCIBLE #18

Justin M.

The Important thing about the tundra is that it is full of plants. It is frozen in the winter and melted in the summer. It is in the artic. It has no trees. Predators like wolves and snowy owls eat animals that live on the plants. Caribou and rabbits live on the tundra. But the most important thing about the tundra is it is a carpet of plants.

(*Tundra*, Biomes of North America by Lynn Stone, Rourke Publishing, 2004)

NAME: _____

DATE: _____

BOTH

ATTRIBUTE

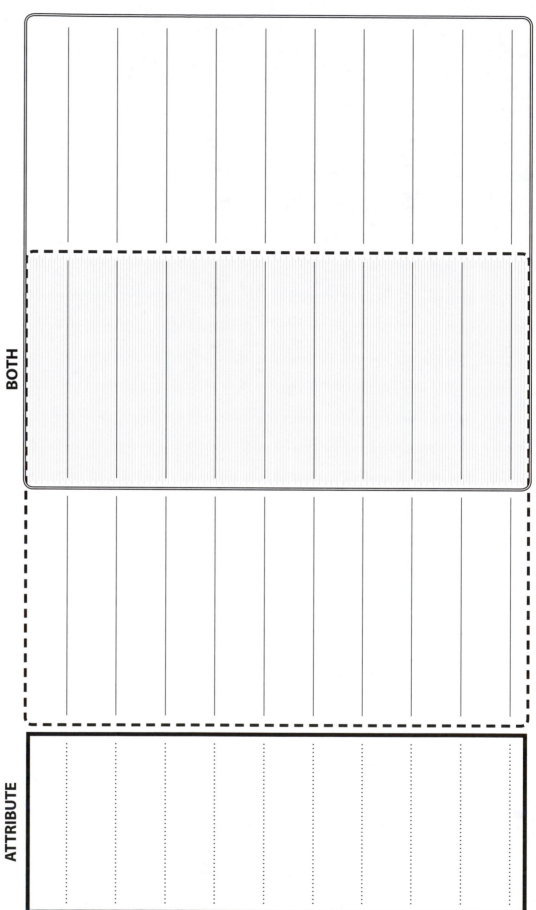

Jasmine

Pairs to Compare

alligators / crocodiles
dogs / wolves
Seagulls / pigeons
pen / pencil
Adding / subtraction
water / ice
Apples / oranges
tile / carpet
Shoe / sock
Soccer / Kickball
Ketchup / mustard
door / window

ATTRIBUTE	ducks	BOTH	chickens
Voice	quack	produce sounds	peep, cluck
Ability to Swim	swim well	are able	swim poorly
Classification		Aves: birds, fowl vertebrates	
Reproduction		lay eggs	
Egg Size	tennis ball sized		smaller than ducks'
Covering		feathers	
Colors	brown, white, varied	many	red, black/white, buff
Feet	webbed toes		separate toes
Body Temperature		constant—warm blooded	
Flight	good at it—high	are able	awkward—low

NAME: _Rebekah_

DATE: _January 20, 2005_

House Salad

Iceberg

tomato, cucumber, cheddar, cheese, carrot

dressing of choice

colorful

BOTH

croutons

chilled side salad

salad fork

very common

Caesar Salad

Romaine

Parmesan cheese

anchovey paste and garlic dressing

green

ATTRIBUTE

Type of lettuce............

Toppings............

Dressing

the way it is served

Appearance............

What it is eaten with

availability............

NAME: Chris W

DATE: 8/28/05

ATTRIBUTE	basketball	BOTH	soccer
scoring	points	✓	goals
action	hands	dribble	feet
running		✓	
team work	hands	pass	feet
where you play	court		feild
balls	rough, orange with black lines, bigger	there both round	smooth black and white, smaller than basket ball
players	five		ten
goalie	none		one
referees		yes	
goal	hoop	✓	goal (big net)

Cue Words
for Comparison

Iane
[Grade 5]

like
similar (ly)
same as
both
also
different
unlike
dissimilar
and
but
in contrast
equally
yet
On the other hand
Compare
Opposites
differs
* Tell similarities first then the
differences.

or
maybe
although

NAME: _Rebekah_

DATE: _January 14, 2005_

the other one

- 735 square feet
- yes, part of living Area
- 4
- linen
- none
- overall - rectangle
- bedroom to the left

BOTH

- yes
- closets
- entrance to kitchen
- one bedroom, one bath

St. Tropez

- 580 square feet
- none
- 5
- room containing water heater and storage room off desk
- dishwasher, washer, dryer
- overall - square
- bedroom to the back

ATTRIBUTE

- square footage
- dining area
- windows
- storage space
- entrance
- accessories
- configuration
- rooms

PRACTICE

Rebekah

    In analyzing two different apartments, St. Tropez and the other one, I have discovered many similarities and differences between the two. When entering both apartments, you come into the kitchen. The St. Tropaz apartment contains 580 square feet, (whereas) the other apartment contains 735 square feet. (Like) the other apartment, the St. Tropaz ~~one~~ is a one bedroom, one bath. The other apartment has a dining area in the living room. (By contrast) the St. Tropaz does not. (Both) apartments contain closets. (However,) the St. Tropaz (also) has a storage space off the deck and a small room that has the water heater. The St. Tropaz has two large sliders (unlike) the other one which has 4 large windows.

NAME: _Rebekah_

DATE: _January 27, 2005_

ATTRIBUTE

	Apples	BOTH	Oranges
Type of food		fruit	
Taste	nutty	sweet	tangy
Texture of outside	smooth		slightly bumpy
Texture of inside	crunchy	juicy	pulpy
Smell	sweet		tangy
Origin		from a tree	
Shape		roundish	
Benefits		high in fiber, vitamins A and C, high in potassium (orange has more)	
Color	red		orange
	yellow, green, pink white inside		orange and white inside

REPRODUCIBLE #28

Rebekah

Apples and Oranges Practice

Both apples and oranges are sweet fruit. While apples have a nutty flavor, oranges are tangy. Both apples and oranges have skins or peels but an apple feels cold and smooth in your hand while an orange is textured. Apples and oranges differ in color. While ripe oranges are consistently an orange color, ripe apple varieties can be red, green, yellow, and even pink.

Comparison Paragraph Text Structure Samples

Lesson 3: Conventional Format: Similarities First, Difference Next

Intermediate (Grades 4-6): Comparing Horses and Zebras

Horses and Zebras

Both horses and zebras are herd animals and grass eaters. They are similar in that they are hoofed mammals. Like a horse, a zebra's young are called foals. They are also alike in that they have a tail and a mane. But whereas a horse's mane is long enough to flop over and hang down its neck, the zebra's mane is short and stands straight up from its neck. Their tails are also **different**, with the horse's made up of longish hairs entirely and the zebra's shorter with tufts of longish hairs just at the end.

Intermediate Grades 7-8: Comparing Memoir with Autobiography

Memoir and Autobiography

Memoir (personal narrative) and autobiography are **similar** in that they relate events in the life of the writer. **Both** genres are presented in the first person singular and usually in the past tense. In **both**, writers make liberal use of what William Zinsser (1987) calls "inventing the truth", for it is impossible for most of us to remember every detail of a past event, setting, or the other persons involved. Nor can we usually remember conversations verbatim. What **sets** *memoir* **apart from** autobiography is its focus on several vivid or intense episodes, rather than describing a chronological series of events over a lifetime.

Comparison Paragraph Text Structure Samples

Exception to the Convention: Each Attribute Compared in Turn

Horses and Zebras

Horses and zebras are fast moving animals that inhabit grasslands. They are both grazing animals. They have sharp front teeth to crop grass and large flat teeth for grinding it. Horses can be found all the continents with grasslands but zebras occur in the wild only in Africa. As grazing animals they depend on their fleetness of foot to avoid predators. Additionally they depend on their hooves for defense. Their hooves are solid and sharp edged. The zebra's hooves are narrower than a horse's but are equally lethal.

Lauren

Practice   list linkin k

Justin Timberlake

◇ N'sync
○ Basketball
□ Tennessee
□ blue eyes
◇ pop music
◇ costumes
□ curly
□ curly, Bounce
△ Here we go

△ Tearin' up my Heart
△ Merry Christmas,
   Happy Holidays
□ 18 years old
○ Shaq O'neal
□ He doesn't like his
   curly hair
△ Cd
◇ concert, Orlando

How to Organize any Expository Paper
(except process description or giving directions)

1. Gather lots of information or ideas about your topic and place each item on individual cards or papers, or make a list.

2. Sort the lists of items into groups or clumps of related facts or ideas.

3. Write down the rationale for your clumping; for example: *These items are all about X.*

4. Order the clumps. Create a tentative outline. Notice what your paper is really beginning to be about.

5. Write your draft in the order you have decided upon.

6. Revise your draft as you discover new ways to make the presentation of your ideas clearer and more logical.

7. Add a beginning technique (a hook).

8. Construct an introductory paragraph that functions to reveal where you are going to take your reader.

*Note that the best introductory paragraphs are written **after** the rest of the paper has been completed, when you know what it is you have said and how you have said it.

Add an ending technique, providing closure for the reader.

Sorting Duck and Chicken Attributes

1. Class of animal
   Vertabrae
   Covering
   Reproduction — young and egg size

2. mouths
   covering
   colors
   comb
   wattle under beak
   feet   ) Description

3. Habitat — water
              ` eat

4. Unique characteristics — voice
                            ` flight

Item #1: Car #1   Item #2: Car #2

♡ light blue
♡ four wheels (white)
O windows
O license plat
O lights
✳ hoods up
O wind sheild wipers
✳ trunk's open
O hub caps
✰ brand new
O doors
✰ instyle

♡ four tires (black)
♡ spare tire (black)
♡ blue car
✰ Old fashion
O Stirring wheel.
O two seats
O pedals
O thin tires
O doors

♡ = Color
✰ = Age
O = specail Features
✳ = location

REPRODUCIBLE #35

Rebekah

Apples and Oranges

Although the cliché "It's like comparing apples and oranges!" infers that apples and oranges are very different, this common saying is only partially accurate. Even though apples and oranges have many differences, they also have many shared attributes.

Apples and oranges appear very different at first glance, although both are a somewhat round shape. While ripe oranges are consistently an orange color, apple varieties are red, green, yellow, and even pink. Once peeled, an orange has a tangerine-colored inside with white pulp surrounding it, whereas an apple is an off-white color inside.

When you eat an orange or an apple, you notice many things about them - some alike, some different. An apple feels cold and smooth in your hand while an orange is textured. When you bring a chunk of orange to your mouth, you inhale a tangy scent. However, an apple only has a faintly sweet scent, enticing you to taste it. Both are very sweet, but an orange is tart and an apple has a nutty flavor. As you munch on an apple, it is crunchy, yet soft at the same time. An orange is like juicy leather.

Both apples and oranges are healthy for you. Both are high in fiber, potassium, vitamin A, and vitamin C. However, an orange contains more potassium, vitamin A, and vitamin C than an apple. Also unlike an apple, an orange is high in calcium.

If you are looking for a fruit that is high in nutrients, sweet yet tart, and a lovely sunny hue, then an orange is what you want. However, if you are looking for a mild, sweet fruit that comes in a variety of colors, an apple is what you want. Both are a pleasure to eat, and their differences make them unique.

Hooks : Question, sound words, exclamation, setting

Endings : Use a universal word (All, everybody, everything, everyone, always, everyday, every time, all the time, ect...)

Zinnnnng. Your reel goes off the drag, going crazy. Do you like river fishing? Well I do. I was wondering because I have 3 great rivers for trout and even some steelheads every once in a while. One place is the... well I can't tell you that. It's my little secret. The second place is ... well, let's just say it's a pretty good fishing hole. Last but not least the 3rd is some where have to in Alaska. You're gonna figure that out yourself. That's my secret pike and wall eye hole. Every single day I go to me my holes and everyone wants to come with but nobody will every be able to learn about my secret fishing holes.

CraftPlus® LESSON PLAN TEMPLATE

Objective (Target Skill):

Genres to which the skill can be applied:

Time parameters:

Materials:

Literature Model Sources:

Procedure

REPRODUCIBLE #38